C0-BGQ-002

JUNGLE QUEST

EDWARD WEYER, Jr.

JUNGLE QUEST

With photographs by the author

HARPER & BROTHERS
NEW YORK

JUNGLE QUEST

Printed in the United States of America

FIRST EDITION

A-E

Library of Congress catalogue card number: 54-12202

To FREDERICO HOEPKEN, *Engineer, explorer, friend*

CONTENTS

I	Jungle Dreams	1
II	A Voice from the Unknown	3
III	Take-Off	7
IV	Scaling Down and Weighing In	11
V	Stork Towns on the Last Frontier	22
VI	Who Said Chavantes?	27
VII	Ow-Way!	34
VIII	Two Visitors from Yesterday	38
IX	Seeking the Wild men	41
X	A Pig and a Ghost	64
XI	Giant Mushrooms	70
XII	Near Miss	76
XIII	My Jungle Brothers	79
XIV	Goodbye to Today	89
XV	A Day Before Yesterday	106
XVI	Eden or Backwash	118
XVII	How Did They Come?	125
XVIII	Race or Place?	133
XIX	My Compass and My Knife	142
XX	Economic Revolution at Ipavú	150
XXI	A Thief and a Free Man	158

XXII Barefooted Ambassador 173
XXIII Which Way the Trail? 184
XXIV The Meek and the Mighty 195

Three groups of illustrations will be found on pages 53-60
93-100
165-172

ACKNOWLEDGMENTS

The author wishes to express his appreciation for the generous help and advice he received from the following persons in connection with his journey to the interior of Brazil and in the preparation of this book:

Raimundo Vasconcelos de Aboim
Horace Marden Albright
José Alencar
Erika Berman
Junius Bird
Florence Brauner
Gordon Brown
Lewis N. Cotlow
Edward Charles Cudmore
David L. Davies
Elizabeth Downes
I. N. J. Eggeling
Richard Evans
Carlos Garcia-Palacios
Eduardo Galvão
Atherlie K. Gidding
Frank E. Hagemeyer
John Henriques
F. P. James
William Drumm Johnston, Jr.
F. van Langenhove
José M. de Gama Malcher
Richard McAdoo
J. C. McCaskill
Douglas McKay
Jane R. Orttung
Albert E. Parr
Roger Sasso
Harry L. Shapiro
Ruby Simmons
Cláudio Garcia de Souza
Lincoln de Souza
Olivio de Souza
Zygmunt Sulistrowski
Dona Heloísa Alberto Tôrres
C. Redfield Vose
Charles Wagley
Bella Weitzner
William Arthur Wieland
William Embry Wrather
Harry Wright

JUNGLE QUEST

CHAPTER I

JUNGLE DREAMS

A few blocks from where I lived as a boy was the house of a famous explorer who had come home from South America to die, Dr. William Curtis Farabee. I used to visit him to hear him tell of his travels. The first time I went into the bare little upper room where he lay, there was a half-finished eggnog on his bedside table and one chair, on which he asked me to sit. Ten minutes later we were paddling up the Amazon, tying our canoe by a thirty-foot rope so that the rising flood would not drown it, worrying how soon our native boatmen might desert us while we slept, and protecting ourselves against vampire bats in our hammocks. It was strong medicine.

There were no pictures on the wall of his bedroom. On the dresser there was a simple bowl of thick metal. It was like an ordinary six-inch bowl of brass, but when I picked it up I almost dropped it, it was so heavy.

Dr. Farabee was watching me slyly.

"It's gold!" I said.

He nodded, smiling, and told me that he had dug it up somewhere in the interior of South America. "It's very old," he said, ". . . almost as old as I feel."

The top drawer of his bureau was filled with medals given him by governments and geographical societies in various parts of the world.

"There are so many places I never was able to reach," he

sighed. "In from the Tapajoz . . . up the headwaters of the Xingu."

Having been a farm boy, Dr. Farabee wanted to go back to a farm. My father and I used to take him driving in our open touring car to look for a place to his liking. But he never lived to buy that farm.

His tales of jungles and Indians must have set alive some sort of a magnet in me. I felt it through the years, pulling me toward the Amazon. I also felt an awe of the jungle, having seen what it could do to a strong man.

Being interested in primitive people from an early age, I took four years of postgraduate study at Yale University and became an anthropologist. When it came time for exploring, I went to the Arctic, where the air was clear, the streams pure, and the insects harmless. Yet down through the years, the jungle world created by William Curtis Farabee kept exerting its pull. And so, toward the end of 1952, as though everything should come naturally in its time, I found myself planning to travel to the geographical center of South America.

My purpose was to find and interview an almost unknown white man who had become virtual ruler of an area as large as New England, in one of the wildest parts of the earth.

CHAPTER II

A VOICE FROM THE UNKNOWN

Ten years ago, the man I wanted to find, Orlando Villas Boas, had gone into the region where Colonel Fawcett, the most famous lost explorer of this century, had been killed by the Indians. Orlando Villas Boas had met more tribes of hostile Indians than any other living man of his generation. He had then decided to make the wildest part of South America his home. Rumors had filtered out that under the magic of his personality, the Indians were giving up the warpath.

I first heard of Orlando Villas Boas when three members of the Explorers Club recommended him for admission. Winning recognition early for his courage and his ability to live and travel in the jungle, he had been sent on the most difficult journeys the government of Brazil could assign to a man and had succeeded in them all. When we studied his routes, we knew that we were dealing with one of the really great explorers of our day. We agreed that he was well qualified for active membership, but there was a difficulty. The men who were backing him explained that we could not collect any dues from him. If a letter could ever be gotten to him, he could not be expected to pay because he never had any money. He lived like an Indian, out of touch with the world, and had no interest in money.

Finally the club elected him a Corresponding Member with exemption from dues. There was only one hitch. Of all the things we might expect of our new Corresponding Member, the least likely was correspondence. Perhaps we were willing to close one eye because we could see so much out of the other. We hoped that news of his election would, in time, reach him by native runner.

My interests had centered more and more in the problems of native people facing civilization. Some harmful laws were being prepared against our own Indians, and it would take more than the kind of lobbying some of my friends were urging to help the situation. The American public didn't seem to care enough about its Indians to approach the problem in any ordinary way.

The native policies of Brazil, however, had reversed an ugly trend and were bringing new insight to problems that had never been satisfactorily solved elsewhere. And the more I heard of the career of Orlando Villas Boas, the more astonished I became. Many before him had been massacred by the Indians. In a day when civilized people were finding it hard to make peace, it seemed worth while to look at a man who singlehandedly had made peace with one group of savages after another.

One evening I found my wife Susie with a map spread out in front of her.

"I'd feel better," she said, "if you weren't going all alone. Where is it you want to get?"

"The upper Xingu," I said. (The word is pronounced as if it were spelled Shing-goo.)

"What about these Chavante Indians?" she said. "I understand that they kill anybody who gets close to them."

I knew then that she had dug something out of a book.

"I don't go anywhere near them," I said.

"You go to Chavantina, don't you?" she said, "and Chavantina is named after the Chavantes. Willard Price says so in *The Amazing Amazon.*"

She had me there. "That's right," I said, "but I jump right over the Chavantes. I fly from Chavantina to a clearing in the jungle near the headwaters of the Xingu River."

"Willard Price says that Colonel Fawcett and his two companions were murdered by the Indians near the headwaters of the Xingu," she said.

The subject became difficult to discuss.

Once the decision was made, the sound of parrots in the treetops and the wild songs of Indians were closer to my ears. But I soon found out I was to meet a lot of trouble before I got on speaking terms with them. I was going to have to raise a considerable sum of money to pay for the trip. And could I find Senhor Orlando?

I knew of one man in Brazil who might be able to measure my chances, and I wrote to him. Two letters failed to reach him. A third brought an answer. He wrote that my plan was a good one but that I would have to meet Orlando through an arranged accident.

To speak with Senhor Orlando, I would have to know Portuguese, the language of Brazil. Professor Henriques at the Berlitz School sat me down across a desk and said, "We teach directly. Now, you and I will never speak English again."

My toes hardly touched bottom. I tape-recorded each lesson and played it back at home. Often I fell asleep with the earphones still on. One morning, Susie said, "You carried on quite a conversation in your sleep, but it sounded more like the Eskimo you were trying to learn when I first met you."

The money continued to be a problem. I received a grant of $750 from the Vose Exploration Fund of the Explorers Club. Dr. Harry L. Shapiro, head of the Anthropology Department at the American Museum, set aside $500 for trade goods with which to procure a collection. I raised $1,500 elsewhere. Even so, I was short by more than $1,000.

As the date of my departure approached, it looked as though another reason would keep me from going. I had written twenty-three letters to key officials in the Brazilian Government, seeking necessary permits and information. As the weeks passed, no answer of any kind came. None ever did. I decided to borrow the necessary money and go anyway.

Thanks to the equipment available to the modern explorer and the ease of covering great distances by plane, I did not expect severe physical hardships on my expedition. Nor was my journey to involve any hair-raising adventures—with perhaps a few exceptions. But my expedition was to have its own quality of excitement as a journey back 10,000 years in time.

CHAPTER III

TAKE-OFF

It was just getting light when, after sleepy kisses of farewell, I made my way to the airport by bus, carrying my canoe paddle and a bow and arrow I hoped I would not have to learn to use. I was taking no firearms, simply because it would be safer not to. If I was to be traveling alone with the Indians, I didn't want to give them an extra reason for wanting to hit me on the head while I was asleep. And as for animals, I've found that most of the dangerous ones are hard to get close to. Far more hunters kill each other.

Soon we were out over the Atlantic, above a sea of clouds in full sunlight. I suppose that the excitement of flying far above the world inspires many to reverie. My jungle trails and prehistoric Indians were now just over the horizon, and the wilderness was so close I could almost smell it. I was in a mood to ask what heaven could offer that the earth did not. Ships were setting forth from harbors all over the world; planes were speeding through space to strange lands; adventure lay around every corner for anyone who wanted to find it.

I believe we reach this state of zest when we let the positive side of our natures win over the negative, when the constructive emotions of love and hope get the better of fear and hate. Sympathy then supplants suspicion, and curiosity prevails over self-consciousness. In ways we don't suspect we can nourish the plus side and, by giving it growth, free ourselves of many of the anxieties of life, which often are linked to the anxieties of death. In these moments when our plus values rise over the minus ones, I believe that God has given us a chance to see what heaven may be like.

San Juan, Caracas, and out across the jungle toward Belém at the mouth of the Amazon. Stars new to northern eyes twinkled up over the horizon as we flew south. Then the plane shook, and a tropical torrent slashed against our wings like hail. Lightning flashed again and again, but our motors drowned out the sound of the thunder.

It was now three o'clock in the morning, and we were trying to get down through the clouds to refuel at Belém.

The only man I knew in South America was there, the one who had said my meeting with Orlando would have to be by an arranged accident. We had never met, and I felt he might tell me in person things he had not explained in writing—things that might save my mission from failure. But a few days before leaving New York I had learned that he was in bed, fighting his fifth attack of malaria. There wouldn't be time to find his house in Belém, and it was unthinkable that he could come to the airport, especially at 3:30 in the morning.

Through the predawn mists, the glassed-in restaurant at the airport at Belém seemed to be lighted by ectoplasm. We lined up at a gate alongside it. I could see that there were only two persons in the big room—a woman sitting over a cup of coffee and a wiry man pacing up and down with a short pipe tight between his teeth. The next moment a Brazilian official called my name and hurried me through the gate. I knew then that my friend had gotten out of bed and come to the airport.

"There is not much time," he said, presenting me to his wife. "Do you want to eat?"

He drew his chair closer. "You are trying to enter a region that is carefully guarded. The approach must be made through the right governmental channels. That is not easy in any country. Orlando Villas Boas has the endorsement of the Indian Protective Service; but to get to where he is, you will have to pass through territory that is under a different governmental administration. The two are not in sympathy with each other. Keep your own counsel and learn to wait. You will not need to mention the name of Orlando Villas Boas. You are an anthropologist. When people ask you, you are in Brazil to find out where the Indians came from. It is an answer people will understand. Have you a hotel reservation in Rio? No?"

He handed me a copy of a telegram he had sent reserving a room for me. A second wire he put into my hand asked the President of Panair of Brazil to assist the visiting scientist. A third informed Dr. José Malcher, Director of the Indian Protective Service, that I was coming and asked him to help me in the plans he had already described in his letters.

I was overwhelmed and said so.

As the men outside pumped the plane full of gasoline, my friend pumped me full of names and advice. He was swift, exact. His wife nodded at mention of a helpful friend or frowned when he spoke of difficulties.

A bell rang, telling us I must reboard the plane. He had given me a blueprint of operations, but he had one more thing to say as we walked toward the gate.

"Find a man named Colonel Eggeling in Rio. I don't know where he is. But find him if you can. He is a good man."

The bell jangled again as we exchanged handshakes.

Once again above the clouds, I dictated into my lightweight tape recorder the directions he had given me. A Brazilian businessman across the aisle and a girl beside me who was going to become a doctor and practice in Goyaz were both interested in the machine, and we played each other's voices back on it. The sky was turning light, and we could see the jungle stretching away to the skyline in all directions.

"Where are you going in Brazil?" asked the businessman.

"To the interior to make an Indian collection for the Natural History Museum in New York," I told him.

The captain of our plane strolled back and was listening to our talk. He shot a glance out of the porthole and said: "Want some advice? Go up to the edge of the jungle and look in. Then come right on back."

Approaching Rio from the land side, we soared down past the gigantic statue of Christ atop the Mount of the Humpback and came to rest.

I started at once to locate the mysterious Colonel Eggeling. I looked him up in the telephone book and was talking to him two minutes later.

CHAPTER IV

SCALING DOWN AND WEIGHING IN

The courtesy of people in Rio even overruled the sentiment of national pride. One man I met said, "Do not let your unanswered letters get you down. Sometimes the mail is hard to sort. We have a boat. When the letters pile up too far, they are put in the boat and taken out in the harbor and dropped in." He was talking to me as one would to a youngster who had not received an expected toy for Christmas. Once when I couldn't find candles to add to my supplies, a shopkeeper closed his store in the middle of the afternoon and went with me to help look for some.

Peter Fleming, in his book *Brazilian Adventure*, pays tribute to delay in Brazil in classic phrases:

> Delay in Brazil is a climate. You live in it. You can't get away from it. There is nothing to be done about it. It should, I think, be a source of pride to the Brazilians that they possess a national characteristic which is absolutely impossible to ignore. No other people can make this boast. The English are a race of shopkeepers, but it is possible to live in England without being seriously inconvenienced by the process of barter which rages about you. A tendency on the part of a traveler to melancholy or extravagance need not be curbed among the gay and thrifty French. Self-revelation may be practiced among the inscrutable Chinese, and generosity among the Scotch. You don't have to be a bigamist to go

to Turkey, and a coward can find contentment in plucky Belgium. But a man in a hurry will be miserable in Brazil.*

But it would be easy to misjudge the Brazilians. They probably represent as many different racial and national traditions as any country on earth, yet everyone seems to like everyone else. I doubt that one can find tolerance like theirs anywhere else in the world. They are hospitable to a degree that warms the heart. They are surprisingly energetic for people living in the tropics, and they love sports.

The stadium in Rio is said to be the largest in the world. Football is a national disease. The Brazilian team always wins. It plays other countries in South America, and it *must* win. Defeat is unthinkable. But not long ago, when they came up against Uruguay, the Brazilians were beaten. As a result, two of the players committed suicide on the field. Some said they died of shock. The sorrow over the score was nationwide.

My friend at Belém had put me in touch with the right man in Colonel I. N. J. Eggeling, one who could take the idea in his stride.

"You will need various permissions," he said. "Permission to make an expedition, to collect Indian objects for your museum, to travel on a Brazilian Air Force plane, to hang your hammock in various frontier posts."

I told him about my twenty-three letters.

"It means nothing," he said. "Don't let them give you feelings of rejection. Could you have dinner with us at home tonight?"

The Colonel was a solid and energetic person, a medical doctor in the United States Air Force, who had been sent to Brazil on a special mission. His wife Helen, a beautiful girl, was the daughter of Richard Henderson, who had distinguished himself in government work in the Canadian Arctic.

* Quoted by permission of Charles Scribner's Sons.

We spread my map out on the floor. "Right here," he said, "is where the so-called bones of Colonel Fawcett were found." Colonel Eggeling had been to the spot. The walls of his apartment were decorated with bows and arrows and other Indian objects he had brought back.

"There was a great to-do," he said. "The bones were sent to England. The teeth and stature proved that they could not be the remains of Colonel Fawcett. His surviving son, Brian, admits that they couldn't be his father or his brother or Raleigh Rimell, who accompanied Fawcett. Yet there they were, right near the tree with the machete marks that the Indians said were put there by Fawcett. Nobody knows whose bones they are."

Almost everyone I talked with asked whether I was going to hunt for Colonel Fawcett. I wasn't, but Brazilians still worry and wonder about the celebrated British explorer who went into the interior of Mato Grosso in 1925, searching for a legendary ancient city of great wealth, never to be seen again. Some believe he may still be found alive, but the available evidence convinced me that this was unlikely, or that we would ever learn much more about him than we now know.

The country I was interested in was around the headwaters of the Xingu River and the Rio das Mortes, near the center of South America. Both rivers flow northward to the Amazon but are separated from it by rapids and Indians of doubtful disposition. On the best map I had there were over 4,000 miles of uncharted rivers in an area the size of Washington State. This is probably the least explored region of its size in the world.

Willard Price describes the Amazon water system as more like a moving sea than a river, more like the Mediterranean than the Mississippi. Ocean-going vessels can go up the Amazon as far as Iquitos in Peru, 2,400 miles from the Atlantic

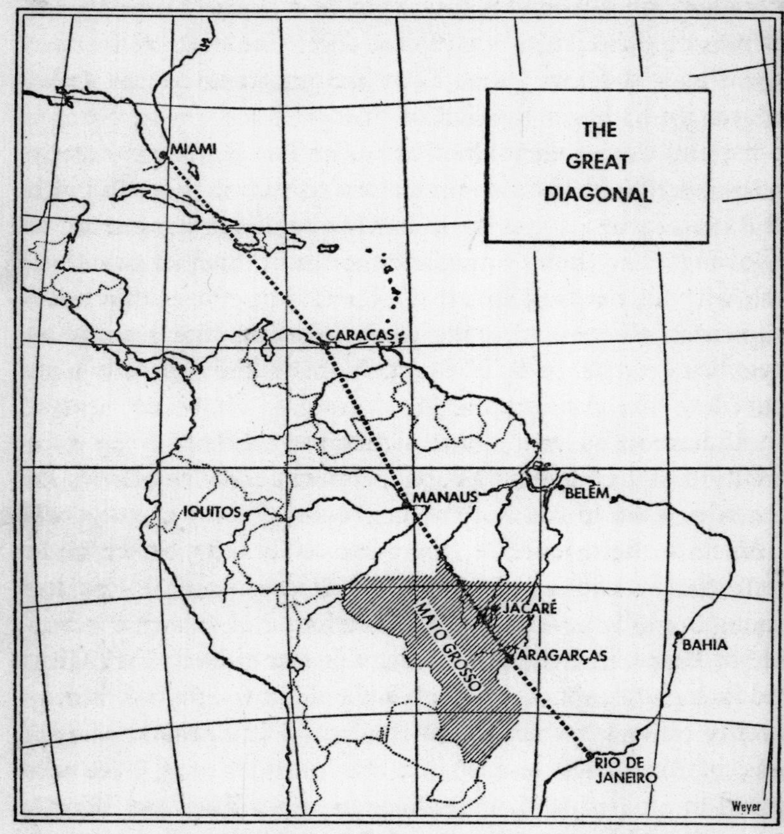

The Great Diagonal is the direct air route the Brazilian Government undertook to lay down in 1943, connecting Rio de Janeiro with Aragarças, Manaus, Caracas, and Miami. The Roncador-Xingu Expedition was charged with the task of creating emergency air fields along this route, and it was on this expedition that Orlando Villas Boas first struck into Mato Grosso.

Ocean, and the river there is 120 feet deep. Up the river another 400 miles its width shrinks to that of the Mississippi at its mouth. At Manaus there is a difference of sixty feet between high and low water. The Amazon River system drains an area much larger than all of Europe. Most of the basin is so flat and the smaller tributaries so numerous that a diagram of the river looks like the circulatory system of the hand with all its capillaries. If you try to cut across the rivers, instead of following along them, you cannot go many miles in one direction without needing a dugout. The land between the rivers is in many places completely wild. Over large areas no white man has ever set foot. If Europe's roads and railroads were moved to the Amazon Basin, a hundred thousand bridges would have to be built. Some of them would have to be from twenty to a hundred miles long, otherwise their ends would be under water in the rainy season.

At its western extreme, the Amazon is only eighty miles from the Pacific Ocean, and the temperature is freezing among the lofty peaks on its higher tributaries. But that is outside of Brazil, in Peru. All of Brazil is east of New York City, and its highest mountain, Pico da Bandeira (9,462 ft.), is only seventy miles from the Atlantic Ocean. The second highest peak in Brazil is Roraima (9,219 ft.), which may have suggested to Sir Arthur Conan Doyle his story *The Lost World.* It is on the Venezuela-Guiana border of Brazil.

The place I was trying to reach was in the southern reaches of the Amazon Basin, approximately 1,000 miles from the sea in all directions. The land there is flat and of moderate elevation, much of it around 1,000 feet. I was aiming for the large interior state of Mato Grosso. It is almost twice as large as Texas but has less than one-fifth as many inhabitants as Brooklyn. Much of it remains unexplored because the region is difficult to reach from any direction. From either side, the traveler must cut across many rivers, and the distances are great. From the south it is necessary to cross the watershed from the Parana River—not mountainous country but rough and wild. This was the route followed by Colonel Fawcett and also by Dyott and the ill-fated de Winton in searching for Fawcett.

"Orlando Villas Boas travels over a lot of wild country," the Colonel said. "He's supposed to be up a tributary of the Kuluene, but when you get there he may be two hundred miles away. Time is your enemy."

So was weight. Space on army planes being scarce, I had to get along with two thirds of the equipment I had brought. I cut out much of my camping gear and dehydrated foods but kept my essential trade goods and recording equipment.

I went to see Eduardo Galvão, an anthropologist working for the Indian Protective Service. His advice was the essence of practicality. He told me the size of fishhooks the Indians would want and the kind of cords and knives that were most in demand in the jungle. You couldn't get along without blue beads of a certain size, which could be bought only at one place, where they cost $25 a kilo.

Besides the things already listed, my trade goods included bubble-blowing fluid for the children, balloons, yo-yos, various colored ribbons, combs, mirrors, hooks to hang things on, soap-bubble pipes, soap, compasses, plastic bags to keep things dry, aerosol bombs, nylon fishline, a swimming mask for seeing under water, nylon rope, skin paint such as clowns color their faces with, silver dust that actresses put on their hair, matches, waterproof match containers, bottles of insect repellent, snakebite kits, emergency fishing kits, large knives, salt, string, two small 20-power telescopes, a 10-power pair of midget binoculars, and some cloth.

There was no argument with the people at the Indian Protective Service over my not carrying a gun. It is the rule in

Brazil, "Die if you must, but never shoot an Indian." This law was established almost entirely through the effort and inspiration of General Cândido Rondon, one of the great humanitarians of our day. A few days later Galvão took me to meet him.

General Rondon is a national hero. Government officials come and go, but he has been admired throughout half a century. His early career among the Indians gives him a sort of glamour. He is a patriot above politics and an army man whose whole career has been toward peacemaking.

He told me how as a colonel, in 1913, he had been chosen among all other frontier army men of Brazil to lead ex-President Theodore Roosevelt on his famous expedition to the River of Doubt. Roosevelt, in his book on the expedition, wrote:

> Colonel Rondon is not simply an "officer and a gentleman" in the sense that is honorably true of the best army officers in every good military service. He is also a peculiarly hardy and competent explorer, a good field naturalist, a scientific man, a student and a philosopher. With him the conversation ranged from jaguar-hunting and the perils of exploration in the "matto grosso," the great wilderness, to Indian anthropology, to the dangers of a purely materialistic industrial civilization, and to Positivist morality. The Colonel's Positivism was in very fact to him a religion of humanity, a creed which bade him be just and kindly and useful to his fellow men . . .*

Around the turn of the century, Rondon had foreseen that all the Indians would be killed if the white man were not prevented from exterminating them. He set out to reverse the entire policy, indeed the attitude of the nation. By 1905, he had begun his campaign for peace with the Indians, and by

* Quoted from *Through the Brazilian Wilderness* by courtesy of Charles Scribner's Sons.

1910 he had established the rule that one would find no comfort in court in Brazil if he drew a gun on any Indian, even in self-defense. The principle that a soft answer will turn away wrath has not been so dramatically tried in any other land. General Rondon himself has been twice wounded with arrows. He was the second person ever to win the medal of the Explorers Club, the first being Admiral Peary, the discoverer of the North Pole. He is also the only living person whose bust stands in the American Museum of Natural History.

During these last days of preparation, I was helped greatly by Dr. Gordon Brown, Cultural Attaché at the U.S. Embassy, and by William A. Wieland, Public Affairs Officer of the United States Information Service, which was supplying most of the more than 1,000 newspapers in Brazil with information and news about the United States. His office had similar working relations with 372 of the 402 radio stations in Brazil.

The feud of which my friend in Belém had told me was common knowledge in Rio, and I could not hope to succeed in my journey without the co-operation of both of the governmental bureaus. At Aragarças, for instance, there was only one rest house, and to stay there required a letter from the Foundation for the Development of Central Brazil. This bureau and the Indian Protective Service both did their jobs energetically and efficiently. It was simply that their purposes were different and their provinces overlapped.

In many countries, including the United States during her early years, people have not worried much about the welfare of the natives. But in Brazil there has grown up a strong movement to protect them. This appears sometimes to stand in the way of progress. The two governmental groups in Brazil who are feuding over this question had become so bitter toward each other that lawsuits were threatening, and the greatest tension existed between Dr. Archimedes, President of the Foundation, and Orlando Villas Boas. I had been advised all along the line to keep my Foundation papers in one pocket and my Indian Service papers in the other.

When I got an appointment to see President Archimedes Perreira Lima and found myself going up in the elevator to his office, I realized I was facing a crucial moment. The Brazilians have a special kind of Secretary of the Interior in Dr. Archimedes.* The purpose of his bureau is to open up central Brazil to colonization, to establish a practical economy, and to make the region produce. The Foundation can contract for work by civilian construction companies, and it is assured a certain amount of transportation by the Brazilian Air Force. In some ways, it is like the Hudson's Bay Company of old.

Making a sudden decision, I handed Dr. Archimedes the official letter I carried from the American Museum, which stated that my purpose was not only to make an Indian collection but to meet Orlando Villas Boas. As his eye ran down the page, I waited for the explosion.

I thought I saw his color rise. He raised his eyes and declared that the work of Orlando Villas Boas was quite separate from his department. Orlando no longer worked for his Foundation, though he had done so on the famous Roncador-Xingu Expedition. Knowing that Dr. Archimedes was powerful enough to throw a monkey wrench into my plan, I tried to talk of other things. To my surprise, he said:

"But you will see some interesting things in the interior, and I shall be there to show you the sights. The day before you reach Chavantina, I shall have gotten there by another plane. It is on the border of the Chavante country, you know."

I wondered what he might be planning for me. But I said,

* It is proper in Brazil to address a distinguished person by his first name, preceded by the title "Doctor."

"That's good!" And, doubting whether I had heard him rightly, added, "I'll see you then in Chavantina."

My trip to the interior would still be impossible without a certificate from a sort of Council for Exploration—the Conselho de Fiscalização das Expedições Artísticas e Científicas. This council was not going to meet again before I would have to be on my way back home.

But there was, I gathered, a power behind the throne, a presiding genius over the cultural and scientific life of the nation. This well-nigh invisible and unapproachable authority was a woman, Dona Heloísa Alberto Tôrres. Bureaucrat and barber, bigwig and commoner, all knew and respected this Amazonian academician.

When the time of my audience with her came, I was led up several broad stairways by a speechless major domo in her castle on Quinta Boa Vista, where she presided over the National Museum of Brazil. If she could not or would not produce the necessary permit, no one could.

As the wide doors swung open, I felt my Portuguese slipping and wondered how I could gain my point in the few minutes that would be allowed an unknown visitor from an alien land.

She looked me up and down and then spoke. "How's Margaret Mead?" she asked in perfect English. "How's Harry Shapiro; how's Bella Weitzner?" She was a modern woman of great personal charm, and she was asking me about some of my best friends in New York.

She had just returned from an expedition herself to Bahia far to the north. We talked of this and other things, and then I said, "Do you think I will get where I am going?"

"There is not time for the Council to meet," she said. "But you will not need anything that I cannot get for you. You will receive the necessary papers within two days. Now, shall we go back to town in the station wagon? I must present an appeal for more money for our work."

Two days later, the envelope arrived from Dona Heloísa Alberto Tôrres. One of the documents in it read:

> It is requested that all federal, state, and municipal authorities, as well as all who live in the land, will kindly help Senhor Edward Weyer—anthropologist of the American Museum of Natural History, New York, who is traveling under the patronage of the National Museum—in the fulfillment of a mission of a scientific character which he seeks to carry out in Brazil.

Long before daybreak, the morning of my departure, I packed my business suit in a box that would await my return, put on a pair of blue jeans and a khaki shirt, and shouldered my trade goods, canoe paddle, bow and arrow, and jungle knife. A taxi took me through the black streets to the airport. The only activity was half a mile away where one propeller of a huge airplane was turning. Men tried to start the other engine for an hour and a half, until the sun had risen well above the skyline. It wouldn't go.

Then, just as I was ready to give up for the day, there was a blinding flash and a large explosion. The starboard propeller was at last turning.

The plane taxied up, and I climbed in, filled with a mixture of admiration and dismay.

CHAPTER V

STORK TOWNS ON THE LAST FRONTIER

To reach the interior from Rio, you have to cross high mountains, beginning with the tumbled ranges that crowd the city to the sea. Like most inland regions in the tropics, the state of Mato Grosso has a sharply divided rainy and dry season. The rain comes in the months when the noonday sun is highest, which is from October to April. We were entering the dry season, during which the Xingu country would have little or no rain. The winds from the east lose their moisture in crossing the coastal mountains, and if they blow more from the south, they have to come from higher, cooler lands and are not rain-bearing. Before the end of the dry season, the smaller streams dry up, and the big ones drop ten feet or more in depth.

Now we had crossed the mountains and were flying into the basin of the Amazon. I could see gleaming white sand bars in the rivers. A month earlier they would have been under water. Now they would make good camping places for a canoeist exploring the region. Turtles would bury their eggs in the sand, and an occasional alligator would come out to sun himself.

The only other person going as far as Chavantina was a tall, thin young man, looking solemn in a pith helmet and canvas leggings. His khaki hunter's jacket might have seen service with Livingstone, and he looked so professionally tropical that I felt quite out of place in the clothes I would have worn to rake leaves in a suburban backyard. He spoke Portuguese with the Air Force officials, but his choice of words showed him to be an expert beginner.

It turned out that Mr. Nagy, as I shall call him, was a displaced Hungarian who had come to Brazil penniless a few years before. He had worked as a doorman in a night club until he had been befriended by one of its guests, a maker of insecticides. Mr. Nagy had been taken into the business, as could quickly be guessed from the varied sprays, lotions, and smudges he was happy to show you. They were to meet quite a test in the next few days. For larger game he carried a rifle, because he was on a hunting trip.

"You can have your Indians," he said.

"You can have your jaguars," I replied.

It was not easy to talk in the plane. The roar of the motors was bad and Mr. Nagy insisted on stuffing large plugs of putty into his ears. His canvas leggings, he said, were going to be too hot in the jungle, but what else could one do against snakes? He was dissatisfied to learn that I was carrying only a couple of aerosol bombs and a bottle of 612 for the insects.

I admitted that the insects would be bad and that perhaps nothing would really save us.

It was then that he let me in on his master stroke—a pair of skin-tight rubber gloves that went to his elbows, which he would wear when everything else failed.

He was a kindly and sympathetic fellow, and we quickly got to know each other. After a few hours, he even had me beginning to worry about the insect menace. But by the end of two days, though I had not used my simple remedies at all, I had not been bitten once, whereas he was a tortured mass of bites and stings in spite of all his preventives. Ticks, mosquitoes,

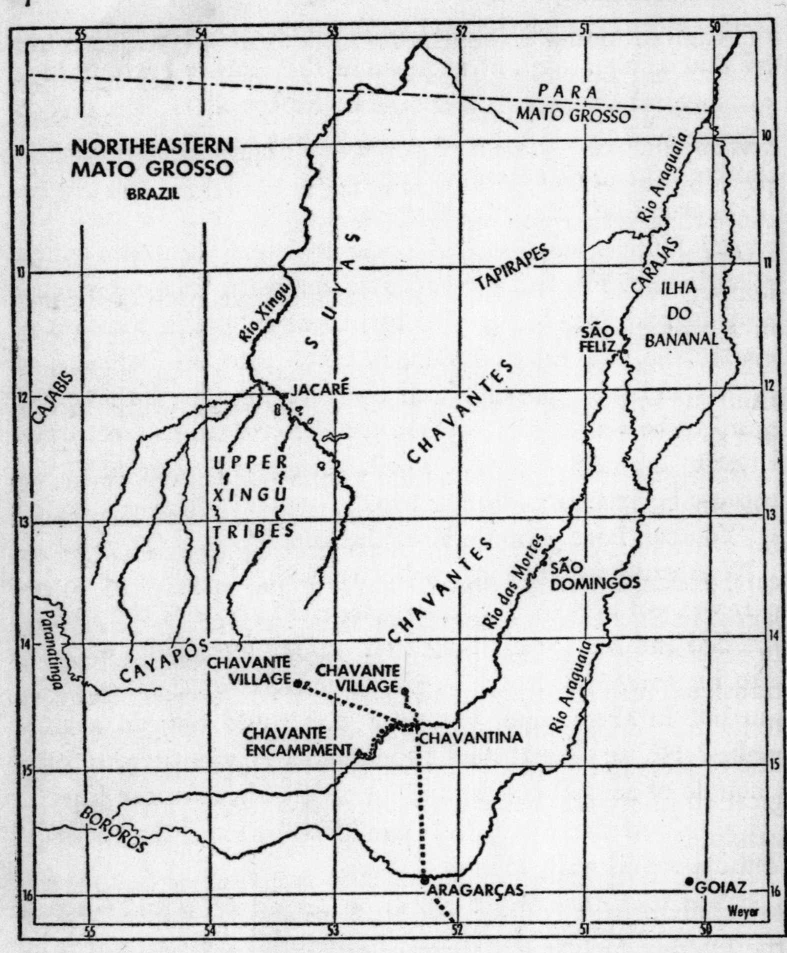

and smaller winged creatures had attacked his arms, legs, and shoulders, even under his clothing, and he was begging everyone to tell him where he could get some clinical alcohol to soothe his flesh. I can't explain it.

Our friendship was short. At Chavantina, he went off into the wilderness with a band of Brazilians in government service. I never saw him again, but people told me later that he got back to Rio safely.

I can best describe the frontier settlements of Aragarças and Chavantina by calling them "stork towns." They have just been brought into the world, and the stork who delivered them was in each case a twin-engine C–47. They were carried in, piece by piece. Only the airplane could have done the job, because they are surrounded by wilderness.

Aragarças, in which we alighted first, amid clouds of grasshoppers swept up by the plane, should have been christened in a pink ribbon, for it is softer and less independent than Chavantina. As I stepped from the plane, a man walked in from the forest with a wild pig on his shoulders, which he had just shot.

Aragarças and Chavantina are not the only stork towns on the Brazilian frontier. There are many others. And they stand for a wholly new method in pioneering. No longer is the oxcart, covered wagon, canoe, or pony the symbol of future lands. In Brazil a young man goes West with wings rather than boots and saddle. The lifeline is gasoline. Every problem is translated into the amount of gasoline it will require. Gasoline to fly the plane, gasoline to run an outboard on a dugout, gasoline to turn the generator or the water pump. This is the last great frontier and the only one that was ever "bottle-fed" on gasoline.

At the neat little inn half a mile from the airfield, I followed six or eight officers of the Brazilian Air Force through the lobby, which was a museum of stuffed animals and birds of the region. We crossed a courtyard, open to the river beyond and noisy with parrots and macaws. In the center of it, there was a water pipe for sprinkling a flower garden. At the far end of the colonnade, we went into a series of three rooms, but I was soon told by a messenger from the front office that I had no business there.

Where could I stay? I asked.

The man shrugged. I was picking up the sack that held my

hammock, primus stove, and toilet articles, when I thought of my letter from Dona Heloísa. I handed it to him, and the doubt gave way to cordiality. He showed me back to the room full of flyers, and presently I was washed and combed and drinking a glass of beer in company with a fierce-looking stuffed jaguar and some pleasant Brazilians I had met in the front room.

Aragarças, many miles from any other settlement, is made up of model houses. A church is going up, and there is a motion picture theater, I understand, but no films as yet. The town was built almost overnight, where two rivers join, the Araguaia and the Garças, hence the name Aragarças.

The airplane has telescoped decades into months in blazing the trail of development to interior Brazil. Whether a region can market its products by air depends upon value per ounce. Diamonds and gold can be shipped out profitably by plane, but beef, grain, and cotton would meet stiff competition from areas closer to the markets. The optimist says, "Brazil can feed the world." The pessimist says, "Future? Yes, Brazil will always have a future."

CHAPTER VI

WHO SAID CHAVANTES?

Before daybreak we had our coffee and bread by candlelight on the covered porch of the court. The Air Force officers took a friendly interest in my plan. They were impressed that I should have made such an effort to learn Portuguese. What could I have done without it? Outside of Rio, I didn't meet one person who could speak English.

Chavantina, where I was flown later that day, is tough and self-reliant, as a youngster should be who is going to have to look out for himself. When the stork brought Chavantina in and set it down on the banks of the Rio das Mortes, there could be do doubt that the new arrival was a boy.

About 200 miles to the northwest, somewhere along one of the feeders of the Xingu, was the man I had come to find. The country in between, a wilderness as large as Vermont and New Hampshire combined, was the homeland of the Chavantes.

The Chavantes and the Motilones are the two most notorious tribes in South America. The Motilones, in western Venezuela, have for decades killed those who tried to enter their territory. One of the oil companies ran into so much trouble that they gave up hope of exploring the area. Then the American Museum became interested in trying to get a Motilone collection. The man they chose for the job stayed down there eight months. When he came back, the only

Motilone object he had was an arrow they had shot into his boat.

The Chavantes are much more numerous and cover a much larger area than the Motilones. About three centuries ago a band of adventurers in search of gold or diamonds reached the banks of the then unknown Rio das Mortes and tried to cross it. The Chavantes defeated them, and there was great loss of life. The river is said to have flowed red with blood for two days and was named the River of Death. Down through the centuries, no one succeeded in challenging the independence of the Chavantes, and their name became a symbol of treachery and cruelty.

In more recent years, many explorers lost their lives trying to enter the Chavantes' territory and the headwaters of the northward flowing Xingu River to the west. Most of them passed from the scene without leaving a ripple on the pages of history. One man—Colonel Percy H. Fawcett—received all the fame, perhaps because he was searching for the impossible. He thought he could discover ruins older and more magnificent than those of ancient Egypt. He was looking for a fabulous city of great wealth in a range of mountains that didn't exist, and he has become known throughout the civilized world. In 1925, in company with his son Jack and Raleigh Rimell, he approached this region from the southwest, and none of the three ever came out alive. It is believed that they were murdered near the western border of the Chavante country, probably by Indians of the Kalapalo tribe.

In the early thirties two priests started out on the Rio das Mortes to Christianize the Chavantes. Their remains were found in the river, mutilated by clubs. They were holding their crucifixes, and their hands had been shot with arrows.

In earlier centuries, Brazil's attitude toward her Indians was not very different from our own, in which men went out to hunt the weakly armed natives exactly as they would animals. The atrocities committed in almost every part of South America have built up a spirit of hostility in the Indians, which still exists in many places where they have not been killed or beaten beyond hope.

Shortly after the turn of the century, as mentioned earlier, General Cândido Rondon, the great advocate of the Indians, succeeded in reversing Brazilian policy and making it illegal to use firearms in the Indian country.

One of the most shocking incidents occurred in 1941, when Dr. Genésio Pimentel Barbosa, working for the Indian Protective Service, tried to make peace with the Chavantes. From a post called São Domingos, about 100 miles downstream from Chavantina, he led his squad of peacemakers into Chavante territory. Making a shelter for his companions and himself, he sent his three Indians ahead to invite the Chavantes to come and receive his gifts.

The Indian messengers hid themselves near the Chavante encampment to listen and make sure that their Sherente dialect could be understood. Having satisfied themselves on this point, they approached and invited the Chavantes to come. The Chavantes spoke not one word in answer.

Upon returning to Barbosa, the Sherente messengers were directed to try again. They did so, but came back with the same report.

On November 6, while they were gone the third time, about 300 Chavantes attacked Barbosa and his five white companions. The officials of the Indian Service in Rio had been expecting the announcement of a resounding success. Instead they received word of the frightful disaster in the following telegram from an agent in Leopoldina:

> I communicate to you with immense sorrow the arrival here yesterday of deputy Feliciano Oldra of the group for contacting

the Chavantes under the leadership of Dr. Genésio Pimentel Barbosa and including Joaquim Guedes Mendes, Fredolino Torres, and Luiz Américo Moreira. Feliciano states that Domingos de Freitas Carvalho and Oscar Grecoviack were 100 meters away from the encampment gathering wood on Dr. Pimentel's order, when an attack was made, and the informant presumes that they also have been killed. Feliciano escaped in company with three Sherente Indians because they had gone on a reconnaissance on the order of Adjutant Pimentel. On returning at night they found the camp destroyed, the bodies in a naked condition. Under each body they found a war club; behind the cooking place, also destroyed, there were a lot of clubs as final warning to those who survived. Feliciano traveled to Leopoldina, leaving the three Sherentes in São Domingos. All four survivors are suffering from poisoning from poisoned fruits placed by the Chavantes at the spot where the presents were left. The Sherentes are out of danger. Feliciano went with me to Goiaz to seek medical treatment. The bodies are unburied at the point of attack. I took care to secure a formal statement from Feliciano, which I am sending you today by air. I informed the Chief of Police.

Marks of machete blades on the war clubs left by the Indians showed that there had been a struggle, but Barbosa and his men had not removed the guns that lay in a box right beside them. They were martyrs to the new law: "Die if necessary but never kill."

There have not been many more dramatic examples of turning the other cheek in our time. For about a month after this massacre, some 200 Chavantes camped close to the river bank ready to murder anyone who tried to come back into their territory. It was not possible to recover the bodies for six months. They are now buried in a little cemetery at São Domingos, where the government post has been named Pimentel Barbosa in his honor.

To Francisco Meireles more than anyone else should go the credit for pacifying the northern Chavantes. In 1945, with ten helpers, he made his first penetration into Chavante country. He prepared four spots at varying distances from the river at which to leave presents. In his effort to soften the hearts of the Chavantes, he had tried to think of everything they would like best: food, knives, pots and pans, even pin-up photographs of movie stars. The Chavantes may have been watching him, for they can hide only fifteen feet from where one passes without his knowing they are there.

At first the presents remained untouched. There was nothing unexpected in this; it was good enough that they had not been smashed by war clubs as had happened before. But after about six months, the presents began to disappear. In April of 1946, while workmen were building a hut at a place called Roça, metal tools they had been using disappeared. On one occasion, at the station nearest the river, arrows were received from a few Chavantes in exchange for gifts, and on the last day of July, when Meireles went to Roça, he met about ten Chavantes. This was the first official contact with the people. One week later, at the beginning of August, he went in from the river again, and on the second day his muleteers, while searching for lost animals, sighted Indians. Continuing to the place where Barbosa had been murdered, Meireles found paths that the Chavantes had made so they could retreat quickly in case of need. He left presents and withdrew to eat lunch. By the time he and his men returned, the presents had disappeared. Meireles then discovered three arrows with broken points. This looked like a sign of peace; and when he and his men called out, about ten Indians came out of the forest.

This number quickly swelled to about seventy, and Meireles began to hand out his presents. But the number of Chavantes continued to grow, and signs of unfriendliness were seen. When the presents were almost gone, Meireles made a fire, hoping to summon assistance. The Indians were growing angry, and he ordered the horses saddled for a quick getaway. The circle of Indians had closed around them.

Lincoln de Souza gives a dramatic account of this event in his recent book, *Entre os Xavantes do Roncador.** The meeting ended with open hostility. The arrows of the Chavantes were raining around Meireles and his men when they mounted their horses and fled. One of them was hit, and so was a horse. Another horse became separated and was lost.

Various other attempts were made to woo the Chavantes, but it was not until May of 1949, at São Domingos, that someone cried out, "Look at the Chavantes!" The Indians had gathered in great numbers directly across from the post where Meireles had worked so long. When he courageously crossed the river and stepped ashore, the Chavante chief, Apoena, threw his arms around Meireles and wept. Kindness had won out.

Two of the many Chavante villages were actually entered, and Meireles kept promising Apoena and other chiefs whom he met that the white man would respect their territory. In this way the Chavantes were persuaded to agree that they, in turn, would treat the white man as their brother. Meireles would have had little spirit for the task in which he so heroically succeeded had he foreseen how his promises to safeguard the land of the Chavantes were to be broken in September of 1953.

True to his word, Dr. Archimedes Perreira Lima, President of the Foundation for Development of Central Brazil, had arrived in Chavantina a day ahead of me in his official plane, and I met him on the banks of the Rio das Mortes. He cut a dashing figure in his boots and baggy zouave-style breeches.

"This is the dividing line," he said. "On this side of the

*Published by the Ministry of Documentation and Health, Service of Documentation, Rio de Janeiro, 1952.

river is civilization. On the other shore begins the territory of the Chavantes."

Dr. Olivio de Souza, the head of the post, was standing near by. "You have to be careful with them," he told me. "Never feel that you are sure of a Chavante as you sometimes do with other Indians."

Dr. Archimedes glanced sideways and said: "You have heard of the Chavantes. Now you shall see them! We'll cross the river in a dugout and try to get to a Chavante village fifteen or twenty miles in."

"When?" I asked. I was thinking of Orlando Villas Boas and the work I had to do 200 miles farther to the northwest.

"As soon as you can meet us here with your trade goods and cameras," he said.

Less than forty-eight hours after I had set out from Rio de Janeiro, and while far short of my goal, I found myself being whisked away to meet the one tribe of Indians I was sure I didn't want to have anything to do with.

CHAPTER VII

OW-WAY!

A truck had been carried across the river on planks laid on dugout canoes, and a trail had been cut into the forest. Once or twice the truck had to go through marshy ravines, and we had to build up the bottom before we could get across. Two or three times we came upon encampments of small, waist-high Chavante huts, but they were empty.

In an hour or so, we were approaching the permanent village. We stopped a short distance from the clearing while a friendly Chavante we had picked up on the way went ahead to explain our arrival. A few minutes later he signaled to us and we went into the village.

No one with a fragment of curiosity about his fellow man can enter a village of naked, Stone Age Indians without an unforgettable thrill. That they may be hostile does not lessen the effect. Men, women, and children without any clothes on and with bows and arrows in their hands streamed out of their dome-shaped huts as we approached. Then they stopped and waited. I believe they were as uneasy as we were.

We couldn't talk to them, and there were a great many more of them than there were of us. The important thing was to let them know that we were friendly. So, feeling as if I had been dropped down on a distant planet, I walked up to a man who looked as though he might be the chief. Meaning to show that my heart was his, I patted my chest and then patted his. It was a bad move. He stepped back, frowning. Instead of friendship, I had created anger. Clearly he thought I was putting some sort of a spell on him.

I hoped Dr. Archimedes and Dr. Olivio had not seen my blunder. They were offering corn and knives, which was more to the point.

I was getting off to a poor start, and I didn't want to be the one who started an argument. So I went up to my angry-looking Chavante again and smiled and patted him on the shoulder. Partly because his first reaction had surprised me so, the suddenness of his next response took me quite off guard. He let out an explosive "Ow-way!" He repeated this over and over, smiling and patting me. The men wore only a cord around the neck and wrists and a yellow cone over the end of the penis. Their hair hung loosely down their shoulders and was cut in bangs fairly high over the forehead and back over the ears. The women wore nothing except the cord around the neck. The nearer ones were now returning my smile briefly. They had strong faces and were handsome in a stolid sort of way. Everyone had fine-looking white teeth, apparently in perfect condition.

I walked into one of the huts and saw that, instead of hammocks like most of the tribes of interior Brazil, the Chavantes slept on mats or bed racks. The hut was empty. All the Chavantes were outdoors for the excitement. I distributed some of my trade goods and received a few items, but this was not so much a trading mission as a good-will visit. Almost at once, the Chavantes began to pluck at items of my clothing, showing that they were eager to have my shirt, my jacket, my shoes. Their own tools and weapons were extremely simple; they had little to offer.

I felt a bit sad for these people, for they were already within reach of the post at Chavantina, and they would soon give in to its temptations. There would be no turning back for them.

I could only hope that the enlightened policies of the Brazilians would save them from the worst of the physical and social degradation that civilization has almost always brought to the people of nature.

As we made our way back through the forest in the gathering dusk, I had no idea that I would see any more Chavantes, but the most interesting encounter lay ahead.

Dr. Archimedes had to fly back to Rio the next day. I was sorry to see this good friend leave. I suspect that he had made some sacrifices so as to be in Chavantina to welcome me, and our trip into the Chavante village might not have been possible but for the interest he took in my visit.

Bats flew around all night in my mud-brick cottage at Chavantina. On the chance that they might be vampires, which carry rabies in certain parts of South America, I kept myself well wrapped up and was especially careful not to let my feet stick out, for that is where the vampires usually do their work. They start the flow of blood with their teeth and then hover in the air as they gorge themselves. There was no way to keep the bats out. They came and went freely through the space below the eaves all around my room. But the people finally convinced me that they were harmless ones.

Chavantina is actually a healthful spot. The mosquitoes are not numerous, and they are apparently not the malarial kind. It was sweltering in the middle of the day, but the nights were cool, and the plumbing facilities, being new, were infinitely better than one would expect to find in a village even close to a large city.

At 6 o'clock every morning, while it was still dark, the table boy aroused everyone by beating on a piece of iron. At 6:30, we were at table eating our morning roll and coffee, the latter strong, sweetened, and very good, the butter not so sweet and also strong. This had to satisfy us until noon or, when we were off on a trip, much longer. Rice and beans, grown locally, were the basic foods here as elsewhere in the interior. Hunting usually added venison or the flesh of smaller animals. We never sat down to lunch or supper here without half a lime in front of each plate. Everyone squeezed its juice either onto his rice or into his glass of water. Leading an active life, we ate great quantities of these simple foods and relished them. Some men of the post were now away, so there were only between half a dozen and a dozen at table. Dr. Olivio, the head of the post, and the medical doctor both ate in their own quarters with their wives. No women appeared at table.

One evening after I had been in Chavantina only a few days, I had taken a swim in the river and was walking up the path with some clothes I had washed when I met two strange Indians. I was in a hurry to put my laundry in my room and get to dinner, but the wild appearance of these two men stopped me short. Their uncut hair hung down their backs, and the face paint on one of them told that they were fresh from the jungle. They had the typical Chavante haircut, with bangs straight back above the ears. Something in the way they met my eyes gave me a hint that I was looking at a pair of men who had no knowledge of civilization or the white man.

I smiled and walked toward them.

CHAPTER VIII

TWO VISITORS FROM YESTERDAY

I was trying to make friends with these two Chavantes when I heard Dr. Olivio's voice: "I see you have found them. This is their first contact with civilization."

"Wonderful," I said. "Where are they from?"

"The padre picked them up on this side of the river, upstream," said Dr. Olivio. "The Chavantes we saw in the village have occasional contact with the people of this post. But these two are from out of the wilderness. We can't get them to eat anything."

Natives who have not seen white people are not easy to find. I doubt that there are any left in Africa. Even when I was in the Arctic twenty-five years ago, there probably were no Eskimos left who were unacquainted with the white man and his ways. In the center of New Guinea there may be a few untouched natives. There are quite a few in this part of South America. Several thousand Chavantes lived in the vast wilderness to the west and northwest of where we were, and most of them have never seen a white person, unless through the leaves from a hiding place.

These two Chavantes were probably in their late teens. They were vigorous and seemed to be in excellent health. Their gleaming teeth were strong and even. They used their jaws as a sort of third hand. I saw one of them bite an eighth-inch cord right in two. Each of them had four or five rows of string wrapped around each wrist and ankle. Their arms were freshly scratched in eight or ten parallel rows, probably the result of some ceremonial observance.

They were without their bows and arrows, from which the Chavante is almost never separated, and I felt no uneasiness in their presence.

"*Peek-a-doe! Peek-a-doe!*" the older of the two kept whispering as he made cautious movements toward my trouser pocket. He wanted to see the shiny Leica camera I had there. I was afraid he might drop it, so instead I showed him knives, pens, pencils, keys, safety pins—all the commonest things—and they perplexed and astonished him. I produced a couple of mirrors and gave one to each Chavante. They were delighted.

When we gathered around the rough board table for our evening meal, the two Chavantes quickly showed their distrust of our foods. They grumbled and mumbled like fussy old maids who thought they had something wrong with their stomachs. Roast meat, we gathered, was their dish, and they wouldn't settle for anything else. They didn't know what a spoon or a plate or a glass was. They were more interested in their table knives than anything else, and while we ate our soup and rice and beans, they went right to work cutting pieces of wood from the backs of their chairs. During the next two or three meals, hunger got the better of them, and they were willing to try some of our foods.

The younger of these two wild Indians had arrived with a large mouth painted on his face. When it began to wear off, he watched it anxiously in his new mirror. Since he had left his compact at home, he couldn't do anything about it. Maybe these two also missed their womenfolk. As the second day wore on, they began to motion with their arms in the direction from which they had come. Evidently they wanted to go back to their own people, somewhere in the tangled wilderness up the Rio das Mortes.

If we could follow them, they would take us to a prehistoric scene, back of beyond, where today is a distant yesterday. There we could see the wild tribesmen living on much the same level as our ancestors did 10,000 or 20,000 years ago. I ventured to remark to the chief of the post: "How can you let them go without following them?"

He made no reply, but that evening he sent for me and said that if I were willing, we would try to go with the Chavantes and establish contact with their people. We would make the first half of the journey by plane, the second half by dugout.

As one of the men at the post said of the events that followed, "Life has its surprises. For eight years the Brazilian authorities have tried to establish contact with the group from which these two came, yet a few days after you reach Mato Grosso the chance is yours."

CHAPTER IX

SEEKING THE WILD MEN

Before sun-up we were ready for the journey upriver to find the wild Chavantes. The plane that was to take us part way was a little one, mothlike in comparison to the C-47 that had brought me here. My cameras and tape recorder alone weighed thirty-five pounds, and I was afraid the plane might not be able to lift us. My pocket scales came in handy. The pilot figured everything and said it would be all right. But when Dr. Olivio, the padre, and I crowded into the plane and it waddled slowly down the strip, I couldn't believe that we would make the take-off. We flew with our wheels just touching the ground for a long time. Then, of a sudden, we climbed steeply up over the treetops.

We were traveling ahead by plane to a little clearing up the Rio das Mortes in order to enlist the help of Teofilo, a frontiersman living at the halfway point. A dugout with an outboard was to follow close behind, bringing our two wild Chavantes and the son of the chief from the village we had visited earlier. From there we would all proceed together by canoe up the river to the encampment of the wild Chavantes.

Even quite close to Teofilo's clearing where we were to land, I looked down and saw twenty-seven tiny one- or two-man Chavante shelters such as are used by roving bands when they are away from their regular villages. They were set in the form of a rough W. No Indians were in sight.

We landed, and it was perhaps a quarter of a mile through

scrubby jungle growth to the lonely little group of thatched huts at the river's edge. Some of the most savage country on the face of the earth lay on three sides of us. Across the river another almost illimitable wilderness extended for hundreds of miles. On the best map I had, the Rio das Mortes was marked only by dots throughout its 500-mile length. We were fairly close to the center of the South American continent.

Out of one of the two thatched huts stepped a tall, lean-faced Brazilian, probably in his late twenties. When I went up to him to shake hands, he presented me with a beautifully engraved visiting card! Below his name, in one corner, it said: "Araes, Mato Grosso." These two thatched huts were Araes, a pinpoint in the middle of nowhere. He must have had the card printed 700 miles away in São Paulo, where his wife had gone, incidentally, to have a baby. This was Senhor Teofilo Prates Reis, who was to be our boatman.

The next thing I saw was something like the husk of a space traveler hanging from the roof of a grass-covered lean-to. This horrid-looking effigy was a deep-sea-diver's suit, complete with ball-shaped head, lead feet, coils of breathing tube, and air pump—1,000 miles from the sea.

"If the Chavantes aren't afraid of anything else," I said, "that ought to scare them."

Teofilo laughed. "I shall teach them to use it," he said. "I would not be here a moment without that outfit."

"What on earth do you do with it?" I asked.

"I use it for looking for diamonds in the bottom of the river."

"Do you find any?"

"Some," he said, but without great spirit. "Gold, too." He showed me his wedding ring. "This was made from gold I found here."

Then he pointed to two other strange instruments, and

explained that they were for locating minerals. The prospector ran water and gravel into a box through a pipe at one end and took it out the other, while listening with a pair of earphones for noises that would show the presence of various minerals. He said it worked well.

Inside the hut we met Teofilo's brother and his mother, a handsome, capable woman wearing slacks, with an easy manner and a smile that was full of patience and good humor. It was Teofilo's brother's birthday, and she had made a beautiful cake with fancy icing and candy beads of all colors, even bright silver ones, which probably had been brought from where the visiting cards were printed. We lay down in hammocks or sat on stools while they made ready for the party in this remarkable household in Chavanteland.

The partitions in the hut were upright bamboos stuck in the ground. There was a phonograph on a crude table. In the opposite corner, a homemade rack of shelves contained various kinds of crystals and other local stones. Against the wall lay some Chavante bows and arrows, to which were tied a rattle made of tapir claws and a Chavante gourd whistle. The skin of a brown panther, or *onça*, hung on the wall above a much worn checkerboard. Teofilo's spare-time hobby was archaeology, and he showed me some bits of iron that he had dug up. They were believed to be 100 to 200 years old, for the spot is known to have been reached by Brazilian explorers long ago. Seven rifles hung on the wall where they would be easiest to grab. Teofilo had been here for three and a half years.

The party was a great success, with lots to eat.

I was worried about the dugout that was to bring our two wild Chavantes from Chavantina. I got up often to go out of the hut and listen for the outboard. As the afternoon spent itself, my companions began to give up hope of continuing.

The boat never came. Its motor had failed just upstream from Chavantina. So there was nothing to do but go back down the river in Teofilo's own dugout. He went with us. As we left Araes, we were treated to the sight of over 100 huge storklike jabirus circling overhead in two groups.

By the time we reached Chavantina, the evening meal had been eaten, and we had to do with a bowl of soup. I was anxious to revive the plan to go back upriver, but something told me I should use care in pressing the matter.

Dr. Olivio might have more to lose than to gain by the trip. He naturally did not want to start trouble with the Indians. Progress had been good during his term at the frontier post. Chavantina was taking on the appearance of a trim and civilized little village. Unlike some of our own rough-and-ready frontier posts of a hundred years ago, Chavantina showed not a trace of lawlessness or discord. There was none of the riffraff you might have expected. The people were hard-working and sober. Liquor was apparently forbidden; weight for weight, there were more important things to flow over the thin aerial lifeline. And there wasn't enough money to attract gamblers. The children of the community met for school every morning, and in the afternoon any adults who wanted to improve their minds were taught by the assistant padre. The newer buildings were all of sun-dried brick, and Dr. Olivio was replacing the older ones of mud and wattle.

Dr. Olivio had won admiration for the progress he had made at Chavantina and for the efficient and fair-minded way in which he ran the post. The Chavantes straight across the river had been behaving reasonably well, but massacres had occurred within recent memory and one unhappy incident would set back the development for years.

One thing was in my favor. The two wild Chavantes wanted

to be taken upstream rather than go it alone overland. It was a long distance on foot, and the Chavantes of the village we had visited were not friendly with the group from which these two came. I learned this when talking with Dr. Olivio about the advantage of taking the son of the chief from that village, who might speak in our favor when we met the other group. The chief's son was not eager to go with us, but willing. Another thing that favored me here was the pride the people of the post had in the wildness of their Indians.

"You will see nothing like our Chavantes," said Dr. Olivio. "Our back-country Chavantes have had no contact with civilization."

"It will be a great pity if we can't see them," I said. Thinking of the scarcity of gasoline, I added, "There would be no need to use the airplane again. We could make the whole trip by dugout."

Dr. Olivio paused, then pushed the bench back from the table and rose. "Very good," he said. "We'll start in the dugout at daybreak, with two outboards in case one fails."

It was just as well that we took two. Dr. Olivio and Father Antonio Colbacchini, a veteran Salesian missionary, had positions in the bow as we nosed upstream under the slanting rays of the rising sun. The Chavantes occupied the middle of the dugout, while Teofilo and I held down the stern. The river was broad and beautiful, but there were four or five rapids, and our dugout was heavily loaded and logy. We had to pick our way carefully through the swift water, where the current was sometimes eight to ten miles an hour. Our powerful motor could scarcely drive us in some places.

The shores were lined with interesting trees—flood-resisting types of various kinds and occasional palms and palmettos. The leafy wall on either side was alive with the flashing colors of tropical birds. Brightly colored macaws squawked and flew out of the treetops as we passed, and occasionally an alligator disappeared near the bank. At one point, a four-inch spider, which had stowed away in our baggage, climbed up inside my trouser leg. After a few gymnastics I got him over the side without upsetting the dugout, and my companions—including the Chavantes, who had been solemn up to now—seemed entertained by the act.

The Chavantes looked magnificent with the sunlight playing on their supple, muscular bodies, but they did not like to have me take their pictures and wouldn't turn around. I wondered what their fellows would do when I tried to photograph them. They might think that the motion picture camera, which I had to raise to my eye and sight through, was some kind of a weapon. But I was determined to try it on them.

We had extra gasoline in tins, but the tank of the motor was still halfway full when it started to sputter and die. It is not good to lose your power in a river like this one, with rapids below. Teofilo steered toward the bank and just made it as the motor hiccoughed and stopped. These were the heaviest kind of motors, and he had to get into the water to the waist to lift the dead one off and fit the spare one on. It started well.

The sunlight became dazzling, and I rested my eyes by stringing colored beads I had brought along as trade goods. In the afternoon our wild Chavantes began to grow more and more nervous, and we knew we must be nearing their encampment. As we rounded a bend, their motions told us that the place where we should land lay directly ahead.

As soon as we nosed our dugout into the bank, I saw three bare bronze bodies moving in the leafy shadows.

We climbed the bank with our trade goods and presently found ourselves in a small clearing surrounded by ten or twelve grim-looking wild men. They carried bows and arrows, and their frowning faces showed that they meant to take no chances with us. The chief stood between a pair of bow-and-arrow men. There were no women here. The wives had been left back in the forest for safety in case of a skirmish. A fire was smoking where they had been cooking their meat on a tripod five feet high with a platform formed of three sticks tied to the uprights about halfway up.

These men seemed more distant from any common ground of understanding than I had ever seen. There was no nod or shake of the head, no shrug of the shoulders. Something about their gestures and expressions hinted that they had evolved along a totally separate line from ours for thousands of years.

These prehistoric people knew nothing about shaking hands, as I learned a little later when, without thinking, I offered my hand to the chief. He did not know what I meant and began to frown. This familiar gesture of ours had no connection with their world. Handshaking probably comes down to us from so recent a time as when men began to carry swords at their sides. A man, on approaching a possible enemy, would hold out his right hand, away from his scabbard, to show that he meant not to fight. In time, it became the custom for two men to clasp right hands as a pledge that neither would draw his sword against the other. Perhaps the handshake was used with earlier sidearms than the sword; but in any case, it is part of our tradition and has no place in the land of the bow and arrow or war club, both of which take two hands. The distant forefathers of the Chavantes, living no doubt somewhere in Asia, had forked off from the common human stem before anything like the handshake was developed. They drifted from Asia to the region of Bering Sea and crossed over to Alaska. This may have happened before the Great Glacier spread southward over North America for the last time. Their home for many centuries has been in the jungles of the Amazon Basin, and they knew nothing of the branch of cultural evolution that led through Babylon, Egypt, Greece, and Rome to Runnymede, Gettysburg, and Lake Success.

As I went up to the nearest Chavante warrior, I was not going to make the mistake again of patting my heart and then his. I smiled and patted him on the back of the shoulder, and a smile came over his face. The men were still holding their bows and arrows, but as we went the rounds, patting and smiling, the clearing began to resound with the word we had heard at the other village: "Ow-way!"

I ventured to return this exclamation, but the Chavantes didn't seem to like it. Perhaps the word meant "Welcome!" and made it sound as though we were welcoming them to their own land. But I was able to get a fleeting smile from every Chavante I approached.

There was something gruesome, almost inhuman, about their faces, but at first I couldn't tell what it was. Their black bangs were cut fairly high across the forehead and back over the ears, behind which the hair hung loosely down the back. Through holes in their earlobes they wore smooth sticks, looking like five-inch sections of round, straw-colored pencils. Around the neck each had a length of rope, tied in a simple square knot in front with the fluffy ends sticking out at the sides. One man had an open crisscross of scratches on his chest, about two inches apart. Their teeth were strong and clean, their bodies muscular and well proportioned. All of them wore the yellow cone over the end of the penis. Some had sparse pubic hair, some were plucked bare. In some ways they looked like other Indians. They had broad high cheekbones. Their skin was the right color for Indians. Their hair was black and straight or slightly wavy, and their eyes had the Mongolian fold at the inner corner. But what made them look so queer?

Suddenly I realized that they had no eyebrows. Sparse chin whiskers, yes; and more body hair than one sees on many Brazilian Indians. But eyebrows—none. Many other tribes pluck their body hair; apparently the Chavantes pluck their eyebrows. I would know a Chavante more by the distinctive haircut and the absence of eyebrows than by any natural peculiarity of the features. But the faces themselves were unmistakably different from the Xingu people I met later.

The tape recording that I made of this meeting preserves the conversation between our Chavante from the other village and this wild chief. What the chief was saying about us, if it can be interpreted, may tell the Brazilians what their next move should be in this frontier area. Chavante talk sounds more like a series of clicks, hiccoughs, and gasps; but it is hoped that language experts can translate the recording.

When I looked down into the focusing hood of my Rolleiflex to take a portrait of one of them, the Chavante eyed me doubtfully. With the motion picture camera the reaction was the same. They were suspicious, and two of my movie shots show them coming cautiously to get a better look. My photographic work caused no crisis, but the pictures I got show some of the tenseness and unpredictableness of the situation.

I wondered whether these people should even be called Stone Age Indians. Their commonest arrow was a feathered shaft of bamboo or reed sharpened to a point; they had no flint points. I could not find out whether they used stone axes. Many tribes in this part of the Amazon basin do not make them. A stone ax would be so important for cutting the wooden framework of their huts that we can assume the Chavantes would have kept this very ancient tool unless prevented by lack of suitable stone. On the other hand, it is conceivable that their ancestors never learned how to make it. We now believe that some of the early people from Asia migrated to America before the technique of grinding stone ax blades was developed. Perhaps the forefathers of the Chavantes were among those early comers. The modern representatives of the tribe would then be the stagnant relic of an early culture that reached America before the end of the last Ice Age and became isolated in this far-flung region. We cannot settle this question until we are able to study the tools the Chavantes use in their villages and can piece together whatever relics may be excavated from their ancient sites.

The Chavantes are supposed to live far more simply than the other tribes, but our unfamiliarity with them may be the reason for this theory. It is true that most of the things we have seen them with are elementary. They live inland between the rivers and so far as I know do not even use boats, only rafts made of bunches of stems of the burití palm, which they ride like a horse in the water and throw away upon reaching the other side of the river. If archaeologists 10,000 years from now dig up their encampments, there will be almost nothing left to show that they lived there. But certain things I later saw cause me to wonder whether the pattern of life in a Chavante village may not be more developed than has been supposed.

One photograph I have seen, taken in one of the northern Chavante villages, shows a pottery bowl, which may be of their own make. And I procured from them some grains of corn, which proves that they do not spend all their time roaming the land in search of animals. But neither corn nor pottery makes their arrival from Asia more recent. Corn is a purely American plant, and pottery is believed to have been invented separately in both hemispheres. The bow and arrow is probably older than either and certainly older than the polished stone ax. The Chavantes I met had no dogs, but I later saw from the air some dogs in a village no one has entered. In Europe the wild dog is known to have attached himself to man and become tame at least by the Middle Stone Age, 8,000 to 10,000 years ago. But until we live in one of their villages for a time, we cannot know exactly what the Chavantes have or where they should be placed in the cultural scale.

To my delight our jungle friends suddenly sprang into a circle and invited us to dance with them. I was winding up my tape recorder at the time and wanted to record this, so I went on getting the machine ready. Some of the others joined in, and before I could get the recorder working they were all shouting loudly in rhythm and dancing in one direction and then the other with hands joined. The forest echoed with the savage voices, and the performance was most impressive. The dance ended, and Dr. Olivio said I should show my trade goods to the chief, for the afternoon was wearing on.

I had been busy taking movies and stills and changing films. When I looked up it could not have been said by any stretch of the imagination that a holiday spirit prevailed. The faces around us, as I believe you will agree from the photographs included in this book, showed that the Chavantes were concerned about more serious matters than how many bows and arrows they would have to give to get a mirror for the girl back home.

I am stirred by Brazil's policy of "Die if you must, but never shoot an Indian." But I was not looking for a chance to demonstrate it. I was quite willing to be looked upon simply as the sound technician, open to offers from whichever side came out on top. I scarcely had time to realize I might not be able to name my own terms. Through the lengthening shadows, which added an unearthly sadness to the scene, as though we were nearing the end of the first chapter of history,

I could see that there wasn't a smile in the lot. But I was proud of my trade goods, and I swung into my act as cheerfully as any traveling salesman.

I had handed a few little presents to some of the younger Indians, but it was plain that the chief wanted the trading to be done through him. He was more austere than the others. I had counted on fishhooks being a fast-moving item, but these people apparently didn't even know what they were. However, they were satisfied with the beads and matches and mirrors and other things I had; and I was content with what I got: bows, arrows, ornaments, whistles, and various other objects.

Presently I looked up and was startled to notice that, while I had been busy with my trading, all my friends had disappeared.

Who was it who said, "Leave them laughing when you say good-by?" Something told me that it was time for that motto. I swiftly gathered my things together. This was an uneasy moment. People have turned their backs on Chavantes only to become living pincushions. The Indians were looking at my knapsack, wondering what I had that I had not shown them, as I put my films and other stuff back in. When I thought I had everything packed, before turning to go, I went the rounds: pat-pat, smile; pat-pat. I was thirty feet down the trail when I realized that I had left my most valuable camera on the ground.

How I loved that camera! But how smooth and easy the path ahead of me looked. The rest of my journey would be almost useless without the camera.

In the end, I counted upon the Chavantes' having a sense of humor—a supposition, I might say, of which I had had no evidence whatever. Measuring the distance between them and the camera, I said, "Oh-oh!" and high-stepped it back

Radio station in the "stork town" of Chavantina, a frontier post in the Brazilian wilderness. The air strip here is a strategic mid-point on the Great Diagonal from Rio de Janeiro to Manaus on the Amazon, and thence to Caracas and Miami.

A member of the most feared tribe in Brazil, the Chavantes. The author had just given him the beads.

A mother and children of
semi-wild Chavante group i
a village fifteen or twent
miles within their territory

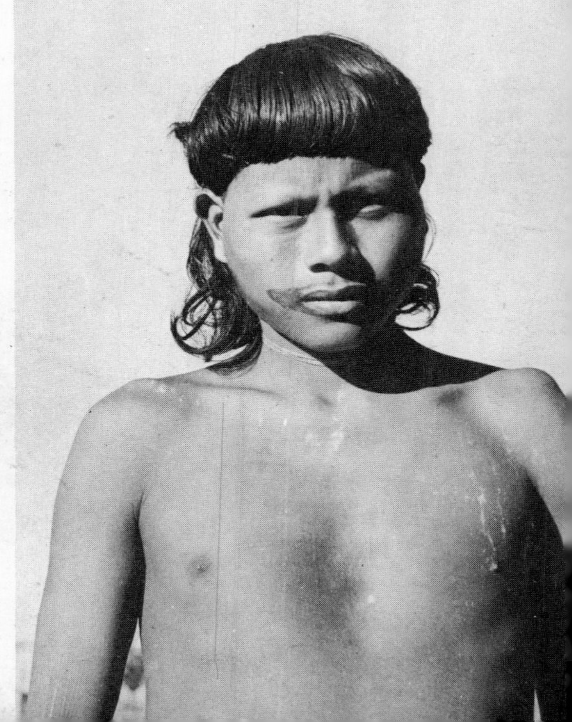

One of the two Chavantes whom the author encountered in Chavantina on their first contact with civilization. This Indian had not brought his cosmetic equipment to replace the painted lip ornamentation, which gradually wore off.

The Assistant Padre of Chavantina emerging from the plane that carried the author up the Rio das Mortes to a wilderness outpost in the Chavante country.

Making a Chavante word list: the Assistant Padre (*left*) and Teofilo (*right*) questioning a young Chavante, who is one of their few sources of information.

Teofilo Prates Reis—frontiersman, prospector, and expert boatman—who navigated the tricky river waters on the journey up the Rio das Mortes.

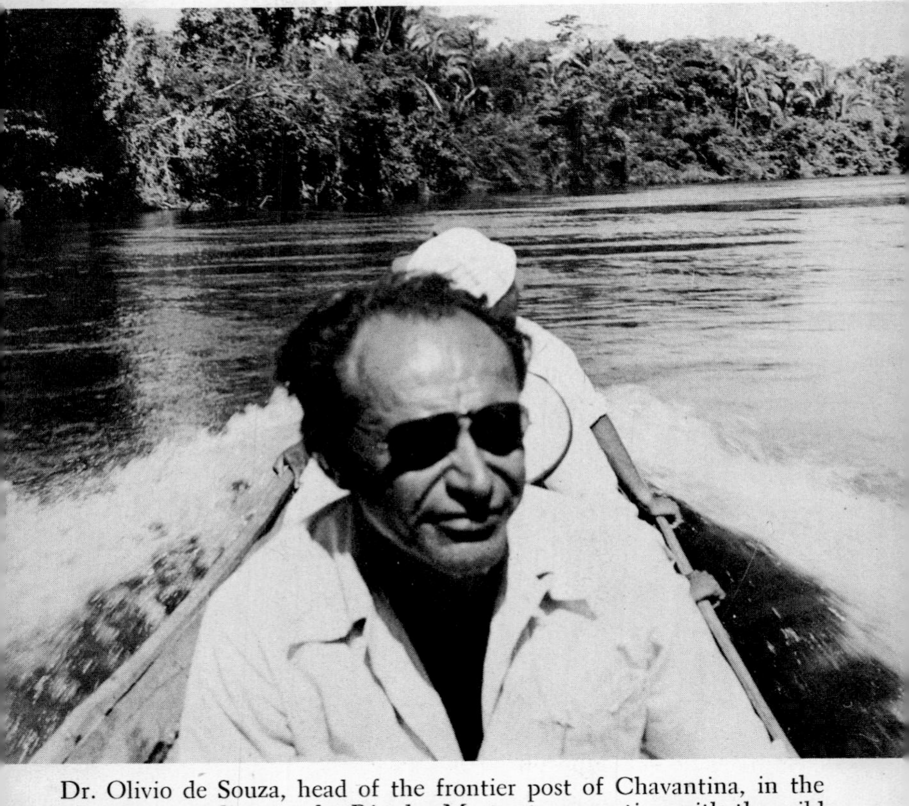

Dr. Olivio de Souza, head of the frontier post of Chavantina, in the dugout proceeding up the Rio das Mortes to a meeting with the wild Chavantes.

The Chavante chief stood between bow-and-arrow men. He is wearing a string of colored beads the author has just given him.

Some of the Chavantes help-
ing the party unload the
dugout.

A young warrior of the tribe who stood near the chief while the white men made their overtures.

Chavante reflects the ness that characterized Indians throughout the rendezvous.

Father Antonio Colbacchini, veteran Salesian missionary and head Padre at Chavantina, who traveled with the party to meet the Chavantes.

Air view of Chavante village never visited by white man, about 55 miles beyond Chavantina. The Chavantes frequently react by shooting arrows and throwing war clubs at low flying planes.

The "giant mushrooms front of the Chavante are racks where the In deposit baskets and household utensils, an top of which they put lo and other foods to d the sun. The racks are of palm fronds and plant material bunche gether on top of a p into the clearing in a pantomime of exaggerated caution. As I picked up the camera I glanced sideways at their faces, and I knew then that a smile is a smile. They got the point and were grinning.

Weighted down with my equipment and trophies, I plodded along the trail toward the river. Over my shoulder a curtain of leaves closed upon a prehistoric scene.

Less than a month after I left the Rio das Mortes and the Kuluene, which is on the farther side of the Chavante territory, fifty-five Chavantes attacked four American missionaries and twenty Brazilians.* The white men had been coming down the Kuluene by canoe from near its source when, on the fifteenth day of their journey, the Chavantes appeared. The white men tried to make friends with them by offering gifts and playing an accordion and a trombone, but this terrified the Indians and they fled. When they returned, the Indians began to steal things and hide them in the forest. In trying to get back the stolen objects, the white men found other Chavantes lurking among the trees with war clubs in their hands. The Chavantes then proposed that the white men join them in a circular dance, apparently just like the one we had gone through. The missionaries, however, feared that this was a trick. They thought that when the Chavantes got hold of their hands on either side, the men with the war clubs would rush out of the woods and kill them. So they broke away and got into their canoes. A short distance down the river, the arrows began to fly. Twice in the next two days the white men were held down by arrow fire for several hours. A slight turn in events might have resulted in all twenty-four white men being killed. Some of the Brazilians carried rifles,

* "Among Savage Chavantes," by Tom Young, *Moody Monthly*, January, 1954, pp 38-40.

but in keeping with the "Rondon Law" they only fired them into the air.

Far more serious, three months later twenty-two Chavantes were killed from ambush. One of these was Chief Suretçuna, a brother of the famous Apoena who wept on the shoulder of Meireles and made peace. Suretçuna and Apoena had been won over by Meireles through his promises that the civilized people would not take the Chavantes' lands from them. Suretçuna was killed by civilized people trying to take his lands away from him. The massacre occurred near the settlement of São Felix, where the Rio das Mortes joins the Araguaia. The day before, the same Chavantes had been in peaceful contact with employees of the Indian Service at a place called Lake of the Oxen. They had received presents and were returning to their village near the Rio Solidão (Solitary River). The men who killed Suretçuna and his twenty-one companions hid where the Chavantes were sure to pass and opened fire when the Indians had no chance to defend themselves. Eight of the Chavantes escaped to carry the news back to their people.

This massacre destroyed years, perhaps decades, of progress, some of which had been bought with the lives of martyrs. The government had spent 5 million cruzeiros (about $150,000) in trade goods, salaries, etc., trying to establish peaceful relations with the Chavantes.

It is a tribal rule of the Chavantes to avenge a massacre, and the few white people around São Felix were quite naturally afraid for their lives. They begged the government to send Francisco Meireles, the famous peacemaker, to control the situation. But there was little or nothing he could do.

"The Indians now have reason to repent having put faith in the whites," he said. "This same thing happened with the Bororos, the Nambicuaras, Caingangues, and so on. At great pain, we had convinced the principal chiefs of the Chavantes that we were there to guarantee their lands and their lives . . . It will only be a question of time until they pay back the massacre of São Felix. They will use every means, imitating the birds and the animals, in order to draw the hunter into a trap. Unseen, they will raid small villages, attacking isolated groups."

The Indian Protective Service immediately tried to make contact with the surviving Indians but without success, owing to their fear and hatred of the whites. The head of the local Indian Service Post, Hugo Mariano Flores, was called to Rio de Janeiro and brought a list of eight names of persons who had had a part in the massacre.

The Chavantes will not separate good white men from bad. If the culprits are arrested and found guilty, it might help if the Chavantes could be allowed to supervise their punishment. In no other way is there hope of regaining some of the faith the Chavantes were finally persuaded to put in the white man.

The Chavantes fight stealthily and fiercely. The thick growth of their forests is in their favor. They can quickly disappear if things go against them. A grim doctrine of family and tribal survival has hardened their hearts to any spirit of fair play. Fear is no doubt mixed with their ferocity. If higher motives exist, they lie buried beneath an emotional pattern that results from generations of determination to stand off all comers, a doctrine passed down from father to son, father to son, and now intensified by the treachery of São Felix.

CHAPTER X

A PIG AND A GHOST

After leaving the Chavante encampment, we made our way in the dugout to a high bank on the other side of the Rio das Mortes and climbed it against a rush of at least eight thin dogs, which were barking but also wagging their tails in a mixture of anger and hope. Between Araes and this place in the river there had not been one sign of human life. The clearing at the top was alive with pigs and children. The talkative Negro who presided over this household, gave an order. We were to eat a pig.

The children and the pigs went into a confused scramble. A young girl with a club in one hand was trying to keep up with the rest of the children, who were hot after whichever pig happened to be closest. As the hands grabbed wildly for pig legs and the club fanned the air, I was afraid a child's head would be bashed in instead of the pig's. The whole scene was forlorn and squalid. It was also noisy with the squeals of the pigs, who seemingly had seen this horrible act before.

I turned my face away and began to add soil samples to the collection I was making for the Pfizer Company to be used in the search for new antibiotics. Here was a place so unsanitary, I thought, that an organism to survive must be a strong one. Perhaps it would ring the jackpot. Anyhow, no one else would ever have brought a sample from this locality.

I didn't know whether it was the pig or a child that let out the final scream. The club came down with a thud, and before

I could turn around, a knife had cut the pig up the middle and its insides were falling out onto the dirt.

Inside the hut everyone was spitting on the floor, and a cannibal cauldron was steaming on a raised hearth built up out of mud. If a Shakespearian company tours Brazil, they won't be able to keep from signing up the woman who was stirring the cauldron for a part in Macbeth. She dropped the bloody and dust-covered body of the pig, roughly cut apart, into the cauldron, then stirred and looked into the pot as though expecting to see the future. Steam rose through her gray hair, and when she looked up she was gleeful.

While ravishing hunger battled against my lingering fear of underdone pork, our host gave us a year's worth of conversation, telling us what was behind the mountains, what was in front of the mountains, and all about the universe in general. There were also a couple of younger men, who I suspect may have had wives resting in hammocks out of sight.

I had been watching out of the corner of my eye. The pot was now boiling nicely, and I was ready to try to keep the old woman from forking a piece out for me too soon.

To my relief she cooked the animal well. And when she lifted the meat out of the cauldron, I was convinced that any parasites or bacteria that had plagued the poor creature in this life were now with its soul in the hereafter. But the padre confided to me that he could not touch the pig; it was too much like eating a recent friend. Wise in the ways of the jungle, the good man had brought along a few sticks of macaroni, which were also being cooked. But that boiled pork was one of the tastiest dishes I have ever eaten.

I did not see the most interesting member of this unusual household until I moved back into the shadows of the hut. There stood an ancient white man, completely silent, against the wall. Long gray hair covered the back of his neck. The tails of his torn shirt hung down over a ragged and faded pair of trousers, and on one of his bare feet there was an infected opening, as though he had dropped a heavy object on his instep or had stepped on something that had gone through his foot. He said absolutely nothing as I looked into his sunken eyes. He was the picture of lost hope.

It flashed through my mind that the fabulous city for which Colonel Fawcett had been searching when last he had been heard from would have been located only fifty miles from here, out in the Chavante domain. There were stories that Fawcett was still alive, out of his mind, in some lonely encampment in the wilderness. I recalled how a Swiss trapper had told the British Consulate in São Paulo that he had found Colonel Fawcett living on the Rio Arinos north of Cuyaba, looking old and disconsolate and dressed in skins. He said he had been wearing a signet ring, which Mrs. Fawcett had later identified.

Could it be that this frail husk of an old man, leaning against the wall, speechless and dazed, was all that was left of the famous lost explorer, the man for whom people of several nations had been searching for more than a quarter of a century?

"How do you do?" I said in English to him, thinking it less melodramatic than, "Colonel Fawcett, I presume."

The old man only pointed to his wounded foot and said not a word. But we had no bandages.

Colonel Fawcett had been fifty-eight when he disappeared on the Kuluene in 1925. He would therefore now be eighty-six. No, the old man did not measure up; he could not be eighty-six.

He never opened his mouth. I whispered to the padre: "What does the old man do here?"

"Precious little!" he laughed, and went on eating his

macaroni. I wondered whether the ancient white man might be a fugitive from justice.

There were few subjects the old Negro had not covered when, with all the dogs wagging their tails, we took our leave. He was still talking as we pushed off. The jungle could not dampen his spirit, and he had a special charm of his own.

The ghost of Colonel Fawcett seemed unmoved by our leaving.

I had imagined that we would camp somewhere on the non-Chavante side of the river and wait for daybreak before continuing the canoe trip back to Chavantina. There would be little light from the quarter moon, and the current was swift. But my friends, after talking it over, decided to keep going.

The dugout took in water in the rough parts, and I was worried about my equipment. When the water began to slosh around the bottom of my tape recorder, I bailed faster. Our dugout, having a round bottom without any keel, wallowed in rough water. After the last light of the setting sun disappeared, it was difficult to tell quickly when one gunwale or the other had begun taking water, and the boat did not answer quickly the way a canoe does when brought to an even keel.

Caution is a partner of fatigue, particularly after it gets dark, and I was beginning to plan how on another trip I would provide myself with plastic bags in which to put my vital instruments, each with enough air inside to float it in case of upset.

Teofilo, directly behind me in the stern, was giving everything he had to guiding us through the rapids. Each time we came near to one of the bad places, he would slow down the motor and strain his eyes in the darkness to pick his approach. Then he would give the motor full gun, and we would ride the waves like something in an amusement park. It was great sport. The spray would fly out ten or fifteen feet on either side. Whenever we started to slide broadside against some of the bigger waves, it took quick action on Teofilo's part. If he were only a little clumsy, we would be swamped. The crescent moon gave barely enough light to see where the water broke white. Many bad spots were invisible in the darkness. It was so dark that I had to feel how deep the water was in the bottom of the canoe.

Then, only about 200 feet above one of the worst rapids, the motor roared unexpectedly. The pin had broken in the propeller, and we had no power. The sheer pin is an inch-long piece of metal that locks the propeller to its shaft. Our motor was now useless and we were plunging into a bad stretch of rapids in the dark. The only paddle was so deep under heavy things that we couldn't have gotten it out if we had tried.

"Have you another pin?" I asked Teofilo, who had silenced the engine.

He said yes, and his hands were already moving like lightning to take a tin box from under the seat and find something in it. What he did next showed him to be quite a river man—even without that diving suit. Before we could fully size up the situation, he had a new pin between his lips, a wrench under one arm, and was in the water holding onto the canoe like the tail of a kite. He couldn't get us to shore, so he was going to keep us right-end-to and try to fix the propeller at the same time.

His head was under water more than it was above. He was playing the part of a frogman, guiding the boat and loosening the propeller at the same time. I didn't see how he could hold his breath so long. Rocks were flying past us on both sides, and if he had been knocked off I don't know what we would have done. But he was all sinew, and between puffs he began throwing the loosened parts into the boat. He would come up blowing like a porpoise, and in would fly the wrench or some small part. Back down he would go with the pliers. Finally, he disappeared with the main nut, and the next time he came up he swung a leg over the side and was in the boat again. He had worked so fast that the worst of the rapids still lay ahead. I ducked my head so he could pull the starting rope, and the motor roared once again. Panting through chattering teeth, Teofilo guided us through the showers of spray as though nothing had happened.

We held on tight and went rocketing down through the rapids, with the Southern Cross dancing crazily over our starboard bow and the Big Dipper bouncing low above the horizon on our port side.

We brought the dugout finally to rest at a fallen tree sticking out into the river near Chavantina.

I fell asleep in my room thinking of my wild friends the Chavantes trotting back through the jungle toward the village where their families were. I tried to picture how they would describe to their wives and children their meeting with the strange white men. I could see them showing their families the things we had given them, the iron blades that would cut down trees, the little sticks that would strike fire, and the shiny things that looked back at you when you looked at them. Already it might be too late for us ever to know how a Chavante woman first reacts to the things her civilized sisters use. Contact has always been first with the men.

I was curious to know from what sort of a village our Chavantes had come. But gasoline is scarce here, and I wouldn't have suggested a photographic flight. Two days later, however, on his own initiative, Dr. Olivio put a single-motor Bellanca plane at my disposal for a reconnaissance flight out over the Chavante country.

CHAPTER XI

GIANT MUSHROOMS

Looking for Indian villages from the air in Brazil is a little like studying the "canals" on Mars, particularly over this part where you can't fly low because the Chavantes have been known to shoot arrows and throw war clubs at planes. We put some presents aboard to drop to the Indians and took off in a westerly direction at 10:30 in the morning. I had fixed a ruled sheet of paper to the dashboard with Scotch tape so that I could clock our flight and record the points at which I took photographs. We flew for about 31 minutes on a course which, allowing for a declination of 10 degrees west, was about 293 degrees from north. At the rate at which the pilot told me the plane was flying (the indicator was out of order), I figured that we were about 55 miles from Chavantina and more than halfway across the Chavante territory when we flew over a beautiful square lake. In a part of the world where shallow round lakes are to be expected, its shape was a surprise, and so was its rich blue color, giving the appearance of great depth. I could see no river entering it or leaving it and wondered whether it might have resulted from a limestone sink, a cave-in caused when rocks beneath the surface had been dissolved out by ground water. Almost certainly, this lake, when some bold explorer reaches it on foot, will prove to be a favorite place for many birds, and possibly the Chavantes visit it to hunt them.

It was only a short distance beyond, perhaps a couple of

miles, that we beheld a sight that was worth coming clear to Chavanteland to see—a huge Chavante settlement in which no white man had ever set foot.

It was in the center of a large natural clearing, and its perfectly circular form made it look like something a jeweler might have made. It did not look like the work of a lowly people who have scarcely been credited with the ability to count above three or four. Father Colbacchini and I both exclaimed in admiration at the nicety with which it had been laid out. To him, of course, it represented great opportunities for the changes he had pledged his life to bring to the lives of the Indians. For me, it represented the chance to study human life *without* change as it may have existed from an early day. The circle of large thatched huts was as perfect as if it had been made with a compass. The Indians could hardly have paced it off so exactly. The circle had probably been made by using a length of cord such as the Chavantes are known to make in considerable quantity for their bow strings.

Dr. Olivio de Souza had flown over the village a few days earlier and also eight months before. During that short time, it had grown from eight huts to twenty-three. A slight break in the radius of the circle suggested that it might have been begun by one clan and completed by another, the second one continuing the arc with a cord of slightly different length.

Chavantes streamed out of their huts at the approach of our plane, and it was here that I noticed dogs. The village had a diameter of about 730 feet, as measured by the height of the human figures in enlargements of my still photographs. The huts were 25 or 30 feet in diameter and could have held from 15 to 25 persons each, making a population of between 345 and 575 persons.

There was one main center, bare of grass, and two smaller ones, which strengthened the idea that two clans had joined here. Each of the secondary centers had a small circle such as might have been made by the feet of dancers performing the ceremony we had seen our wild Chavantes do in the forest.

The most spectacular feature of the village was the long avenue, or *estrada* (highway), leading out from the center for about a mile. I expected to see at the end of it something of importance, perhaps some sort of a religious object, but the avenue simply disappeared into the jungle.

We flew lower over a broad treeless area behind the village and dropped our presents without hitting anyone. We had corn and other food, and soap. I'm still wondering how that soap helped their digestion.

Then we made out a curved row of strange objects that formed an inner circle about fifty feet in front of the huts all around. They were taller than a man, and looked exactly like giant mushrooms. There were about forty of them. They cast as perfect shadows as mushrooms would, and each had a single stalk about half a foot in diameter.

The village was not old enough for these things to be trees. There seemed to be a dark object in the center of most of the globular tops. When we published enlargements of these for the first time in *Natural History* Magazine, some readers were sure that a dog or large bird sat in the center of each. Others wrote in to suggest various ceremonial purposes; perhaps they were totem poles of some kind, or elevated platforms where the dead would be placed before carrying them down the great avenue to a final resting place. Since more than one mushroom sometimes stood in front of a dwelling, it was suggested that each one stood for a family living in the hut. My friend Worthen Paxton wrote: "Have you thought of the best solution of all for the mushrooms? They are mushrooms."

It was annoying to fly over these curious objects without daring to go close enough to see what they really were. Racks and platforms are common in Indian villages, but who ever saw the Indians or any other native people build things with only one leg instead of four? The technical difficulties of such a design are obvious, yet that is what my Brazilian friends at Chavantina insisted they were—racks for household furnishings, cooking utensils, weapons, or the like. And confirmation of this theory came from Lincoln de Souza of the newspaper *A Noite* in Rio de Janeiro. He had been associated with some of the most interesting activities connected with the pacification of the Chavantes north of Chavantina. He himself did not know what they were, but he got in touch with Senhor Francisco Meireles, the celebrated peacemaker. Meireles had actually seen the mushroom-shaped things on the ground in a village he had entered. They were supports made of palm fronds and other dry plant material, standing on a wooden leg. The Chavantes used them for hanging up wicker baskets and other household utensils and for drying locusts, corn, and the like in the sun. The only riddle that remains is why the people would go to such trouble to make a place for things that could easily be stored inside their huts. Perhaps the things placed on top of the "mushrooms" either need sunlight or a free circulation of air. The well-known anthropologist Franz Blom, residing in Chiapas, Mexico, suggested that the single stalk may be a device to protect food stuffs from ants and other insects.

From the moment when primitive people meet civilized man, it is only a matter of days or even hours before they have begun to lose the finer points that set them apart. In this age of standardization, when mass production and almost universal intercommunication put strong pressure on us to dress alike, eat alike, and think alike, it would be a pity if anything so outlandishly strange as that village and its people should not be carefully studied before the people change.

A thing I saw happen at Chavantina will show how quickly the people of nature drop their own mannerisms and take on the ways of the white man. Only a few hours after the two wild Chavantes had come in to the post there, I gave each of them a box of safety matches. We were sitting at the table eating, and I was watching the older of the two. Next to him was one of the white men, talking to a companion across the table. The white man took out a package of cigarettes from his shirt pocket and prepared to light one. The Chavante caught on immediately—this called for a match. But he couldn't remember how to get into the pocket of a pair of trousers the padre had given him. Finally he solved that problem and pulled out the matchbox. His fingers worked frantically trying to open it every way but the right one. He was almost tearing it apart in his eagerness. The man was tapping his cigarette on the back of his hand when the Chavante finally got the box open and started striking the wrong end of the match on the wrong part of the box. The man was now getting his own match, and it looked as though the Chavante would come in second. But he finally struck a light and, with a grand gesture, swung the match in front of the man's cigarette, as gracefully as any college freshman might have done for his girl at a dance. The Brazilian didn't notice at first who was lighting his cigarette. When he did, he could hardly believe his eyes. "It doesn't take them long," he said, and that is the truth.

Dr. Olivio spoke of trying to land in that Chavante village, but before attempting it, he wanted to get some assurance via the jungle grapevine that the people would welcome a visit. He hoped it would be possible to try in a month or two. I wanted to be there when he did, and I should be returning from the Xingu about that time. But when the time came, the plane that brought me developed propeller trouble, and the pilot was not willing to risk coming down at Chavantina. A little later, massacre of the twenty-two Chavantes near São Felix made any such undertaking less attractive.

The Chavantes are not located on the tribal map in Kalervo Oberg's excellent *Indian Tribes of Northern Mato Grosso, Brazil,* though the positions of the surrounding tribes are shown. So little is known of the Indians living between the Rio das Mortes and the Xingu and its tributaries that the name Chavantes may have been applied too loosely in common speech. Any nonriver Indian living in this area is apt to be referred to as a Chavante. The Chavantes are shown on the American Geographical Society map published in 1935 as living in the territory along the Rio das Mortes from above Chavantina to the latitude of the big "island" in the Araguaia River called Ilha do Bananal. South and north of them, in regions 400 miles apart, the Cayapós are indicated, but this term has been applied to any wild Indians in the region. The so-called Mountains of the Chavantes (Serra do Chavantes) are east of Ilha do Bananal, 200 miles from the area usually thought of when speaking of the Chavantes. The map just referred to indicates Chavantes living in that region, but I cannot vouch for their existence.

My anxiety to get on with my search for Orlando Villas Boas was plaguing me. I was afraid that I would be left without enough time to get to him. But it was only two days later that a single-engine plane was made ready to take me diagonally across the Chavante country to the northwest, toward the clearing from which I expected to be able to make my way by dugout.

CHAPTER XII

NEAR MISS

Flying gives a much better idea of geography than the early explorers could get in their canoes. Following the rivers by boat, you see only a wall of jungle on each side, and it is easy to imagine that there is continuous forest between one river and the next. From the air you soon learn that this is not so. In northern Mato Grosso there are large stretches of open grassland with scattered small trees and bushes. Closer to the Amazon, the jungle is unbroken over large areas and much thicker.

We had taken off at 8:25 in the morning, and I was anxious to try to see the Thunder Mountains, the Serra do Roncador, in which Colonel Fawcett expected to find his fabulous city and the survivors of the mythical Lost Continent of Atlantis. Actually, the mountains themselves are almost mythical; the land here is nearly flat. If you were traveling on the ground, you might speak differently of it, but from the air the country did not look very rough. The explorer's chief difficulties would be rather rivers to cross, dense jungles to cut a way through, and especially Indians.

Soon we had passed the thickest jungle and were flying over scrubby country interlaced with rivers that were edged with dark green forests. Sometimes we saw the trails used by the Indians. After an hour and five minutes, we came again to continuous forest, for we were now approaching the Kuluene River, though still some distance from our objective, Jacaré.

The Kuluene is the easternmost of the five rivers that join like the fingers of a hand to form the Xingu in the center of South America. The others, counting westward, are the Kuliseu (pronounced Kool-ee-say-voo), Batovi, Ronuro, and von den Steinen. The plateau they drain slopes from about 1,500 feet at their sources in the south to about 1,000 feet where they join to form the Xingu. This is the land of the jaguar, the tapir, and the jaguatirica; the black jaguar and the puma; the wild pig, paca, coati, anteater, and capybara—an animal of the same order as the rat but four feet long. Parrots, macaws, mutums, and hosts of brightly colored smaller birds flash among the trees. Physical barriers—jungle and rivers that flow the wrong way or are broken by rapids—have kept this region cut off from the world. East of the Indians of the upper Xingu—the so-called Xinguanas—live tribes openly hostile to them: the Chavantes, the Suyás, the Cayapó. To the south, west, and north are others—the Xicão, the Cajabí, the Juruna, and the Tshukahamãe.

In 20 minutes more we were over the Rio Tanguro, flowing out of the Chavante country to join the Kuluene. Presently a beautiful lake appeared on our left, shaped like a kidney bean, with a small Indian village, looking very neat, near the indentation and a small island opposite it. At intervals of seven and one-half minutes, three other large lakes passed under us, one of them at least five miles long. In one place, we passed over a highly complicated series of crescent lakes that had been made when a winding stream shifted its course and left the loops cut off from the rest of the drainage. The result looked like a writhing mass of serpents with their coils partly buried.

Two hours after leaving Chavantina, we saw ahead the thatched huts of the Indian village at Jacaré and knew that we had reached our goal. Orlando Villas Boas' village was some distance upstream from here, on a small tributary of the Kuluene known as the Tuatuarí.

As we came down, the pilot, next to whom I was sitting, began shouting orders, because our brakes had failed and he needed help in bringing the plane in. As we sped toward the end of the clearing, he swung the tail back and forth trying to slow us down, while I, following his instructions, tried to hold the tail down with the stabilizer. We ran off into the rough and kept going. We stopped a few feet from the forest. The pilot ran a handkerchief across his forehead.

Five weeks had passed since my arrival in Brazil, but at last I had reached the outpost from which I thought I could find the almost legendary character whose story I had come so far to get. Ten naked Indian girls swarmed around the plane. I stepped out and, to my dismay, learned that Orlando Villas Boas had passed through this spot only the day before on a two or three weeks' canoe trip down the Xingu River, halfway to the Amazon.

CHAPTER XIII

MY JUNGLE BROTHERS

I could not catch up with Orlando. He had the only outboard motor in the region. My time was running out.

The plane that had brought me disappeared over the treetops toward Chavantina, and I looked around. I was now very close to the geographical center of South America, in latitude 12° 0′ S. and longitude 53° 34′ W.

Senhor Alencar lived with his wife and two infants in a thatched hut a hundred yards away and was in charge of the air strip. He offered me every hospitality, but of course he could not help solve my problem. There was nothing to do but camp on Orlando's trail and stretch my stay.

I thought it out as I walked to the Indian village a short distance away with a Camayurá named Tah-koo-mah, who spoke some Portuguese. By taking a plane home instead of a boat, I could gain more than a week. In addition, I could take up to a week or ten days more than I had planned. This would give me almost a month before I would have to leave the interior. If nothing happened to delay Orlando, I might still fulfill my mission.

In the Indian village, I was soon resting in a hammock among some of Tah-koo-mah's tribesmen. I could only talk to them through Tah-koo-mah, but they showed themselves friendly. It would be interesting to stay here for two or three weeks, but a more exciting chance was opening up. Ten or twelve of the Indians were traveling to another village some distance away, and Tah-koo-mah invited me to go with them.

They were wild-looking, muscular men in their prime, one of whom was Tah-koo-mah's father, Chief Kutamapú of the Camayurás. Some wore necklaces of jaguar teeth and red and yellow feather ear plugs. All were barefooted, and they had nothing else on except a string of beads around the waist. All of them wore their hair in the bowl-shaped bob that is the fashion in the headwaters of the Xingu River.

"There will be dancing and singing when we get to the village," said Tah-koo-mah, "and you can trade for the things we make."

People had warned me that the Indians in these parts would steal whatever they could from a traveler. I had heard of a United States Army officer in full brass who had been flown into the interior on a courtesy tour. Wanting to get cool, he went swimming in a river. When he came out, everything he wore had been taken, and he would have been glad to go back to Rio in a barrel.

"How far is it?" I asked Tah-koo-mah.

He seemed vague. "Not far," he said.

He could not locate his village on a large-scale map I had. He thought perhaps it was off the edge. He was uncertain about the direction.

"Is there water near your village?" I was wondering how far I might have to go to get drinking water and whether I would have to boil it to purify it. Also my clothes were dirty, and I wanted to wash them.

"Our village is on a beautiful lake," he said. "Swimming all the time."

There are two kinds of explorers, depending upon how they look at adventures. One kind doesn't think he has been anywhere unless he has had many close shaves. The other believes that adventures are a sign of incompetence. There are more of the explorers who rejoice in adventures, and they are the ones the public is more apt to hear about, because their stories make the headlines. But the explorers who admit that adventures are a sign of incompetence are a growing group. I believe they are right, and I doubt that one should ordinarily travel alone off the beaten track. An accident, an attack of appendicitis, or the hostility of natives can quickly become serious. I had not made much of an impression on the chief, and I had to admit that they were a rough-looking lot. On the other hand, I felt drawn to these fellows and longed to see their life.

In a situation like this, I know of only one thing to go by. You can't ask for a Dun and Bradstreet report; you can't draw up a contract and have it notarized; nor will Duncan Hines tell you how the food is going to be. You can't call up a friend and get his advice, and you can't expect to take it to court if somebody doesn't prove to be a gentleman. You can only follow a sort of intuition. You watch every expression, every movement, every gesture. But when it comes to knowing how a primitive man feels about you, there is no better guide than how you feel about him. I figured that these were truly natural natives and that they could not have fooled me into liking them if they had been plotting against me.

"I accept your invitation," I told Tah-koo-mah, and we left the next morning at sun-up, in three canoes, to the music of flutes.

Each Indian traveled with his hammock, a bow and arrows, and a huge piece of pancake, perhaps two feet across, made of manioc flour and called *menyú*. I carried no firearms, and I doubt that the Indians would have wanted me with a gun. I had my bow and arrows, which probably made them think of me more as one of them; and I was now happy to have my "sporting goods" paddle. There is usually not an extra paddle in a group like this, and they examined it admiringly. There was no talk about my paying them, though I could scarcely be called an easy load with 175 pounds of equipment and supplies.

Down the Jacaré (Alligator) River we paddled. Here was a scene as far from our civilization as one could find. The movie makers could not have made up anything so lovely and so freely natural. Some of the Indians wore bright feathers in their hair, and the colors of the sunrise lighted the cool mist under the jungle growth of the shores. The flutes continued to give out their fluid notes from separate canoes.

Sometimes the Indians paddled hard, racing with one another; sometimes they loafed and joked. Once we stopped to eat papaya and manioc. A short distance up the Kuluene we edged over to the west bank where the water was rushing past a twenty-foot gap in the shore. Paddling hard, we dodged into this narrow opening and found ourselves in a stream that widened at first and then narrowed. Here men with bows and arrows stood in the fronts of the boats ready to shoot fish. A parrot that was traveling with us as a pet now took a fancy to the top of my head and bit my hand every time I reached up.

The river ended after awhile in a swampy forest. Through this we went barelegged. The boots I had brought were not high enough for the water. The Xingu Indians never wear anything on their feet, but they wrap raffialike lashings of embira bark around their ankles, possibly as a decoration but perhaps also to protect them from snakes.

It was slow work feeling my way along the slippery logs in bare feet. The best I could hope for was that I wouldn't lose my balance and fall clear in. The heat was terrific, and I had to balance my cameras and at the same time swat insects. The region has much malaria, but the Indians apparently enjoy a sort of uneasy immunity to it. The trip was nothing at all for them, of course, and I found them edging ahead of me. I caught up with Tah-koo-mah, the chief's son, and asked whether we were getting there.

"Not much farther," he answered.

"More than ten minutes or less than ten minutes?" I asked.

He seemed in doubt. "Perhaps less."

He didn't have any clear idea about time or distance or numbers.

There followed a march across a blazing plain. There were scattered scrubby trees and large termite nests that stood several feet above the ground. The nests would be a hazard to a plane trying to find a clear space for an emergency landing, especially at noonday when they cast no shadows. Occasionally we stopped and sat on the ground, but it was hard to find shade under the scrubby trees. A knapsack on my back was soaked with perspiration, and the yellow boxes of film for my Rolleiflex had all come apart. I didn't like to think what condition the films might be in. There were occasional urucú bushes (*Bixa orellana*), which the Indians darted off to rob of their prickly heart-shaped pods for the red coloring matter that surrounds the seeds. All through this region the Indians use this for painting their bodies.

In the extreme heat I had been drinking quantities of water, and soon my canteen was empty. This was before I had learned of a tree that grows here from which one can get a sweet, cool nectar in the early morning. The tree bears hundreds of little waxy berries in loose clusters, among which gathers a clear liquid that can be sucked up by the mouthful.

Other interesting trees in this region include the so-called sandpaper tree, or *lixeria*, whose large leaves are so rough and tough that the Indians use them for smoothing and shaping wood. In damp lowlands you see the buriti palm (*Mauritia vinifera* Mart), from which Indians get most of the fiber for making twine for hammocks, arrow lashings, and the like. The jatobá tree (*Hymenaea stilbocarpa* and *H. Courbaril*) provides the three-quarter-inch bark that is removed in one piece by wedges and shaped while still flexible into a canoe. The nut of the tucum palm (*Astrocaryum tucuma*) gives the Indians the sound-making head for their whistling arrows. The bluish-black body paint they use comes from the genipapo plant (*Genipa americana* L.). There is abundant bamboo in some localities for flutes and arrows, and the timbó vine contains a poison that is used in fishing.

I was told that it was possible in the rainy season to get to the lake where we were going entirely by canoe but that the water was now too low. I was wearing my light rubber boots as a protection against snakes and was glad to have them also for an unexpected reason. They left a distinctly civilized footprint that would help me find my way back if, by mischance, I had to make the journey alone.

These men of the jungle were setting a stiff pace. A withering sun was beating down on us, and I had taken off one article of soaked clothing after another until I was naked. I was more comfortable that way, but I couldn't go long like an Indian without severe sunburn.

Three hours after I had last sought information from Tah-koo-mah, we were in our third swamp, wading now to our thighs in black mud.

"Does the padre from Chavantina get to your village often?" I asked him. Chavantina was 200 miles from here.

"No, he has never been there."

"Who visited your village last?" I asked.

"No one. You are the first white man ever to visit our village," he said.

If others had made their way to Lake Ipavú, I thought, perhaps they had gone through without stopping at this village. The darkness of the swamp did not lighten my mood. I had food for two weeks but was beginning to wonder how I would get back through these jungles if the Indians lost interest in me. It was not a trip one would welcome alone. I could not do it with even a fraction of my photographic and recording equipment. And a boat, or at least a raft, was needed at both ends.

We found a large dugout the Indians had hidden in the swamp. In this we poled and pulled our way along by hanging vines. Gradually the waterway widened into a small stream, roofed over by trees, which for lack of a better name we may call the Lesser Limpopo.

Suddenly the trees parted, and we glided out onto a sparkling lake. Around the shore, palm trees nodded in silhouette against the cottony clouds. So peaceful and entrancing a spot seemed not a part of the world we know.

From this moment, I felt that I had reached a hidden corner where time had stood still, a secret Eden infinitely distant in history. Down through the centuries, while civilization had been rushing onward, human life on the elemental level must have been lived here as from the early days of our ancestors, unchanged by any echo of what we call progress.

My faith in human nature, if it had weakened, was now restored, for—wonder of wonders—the chief (who had only one eye and seemed to look at me doubtfully out of it) somehow brought himself to pat me on the back.

What I did not know at the time was that these Indians had killed another white man and dropped his bones into this lake. He was a journalist from California named Albert de Winton. His murderer was a Camayurá who was now living on the west side of the lake, in a village I could have seen if I had squinted my eyes. The Indian had hit de Winton over the head at the joining of two rivers a few miles from here; and when the explorer's bones had turned white, the Indians

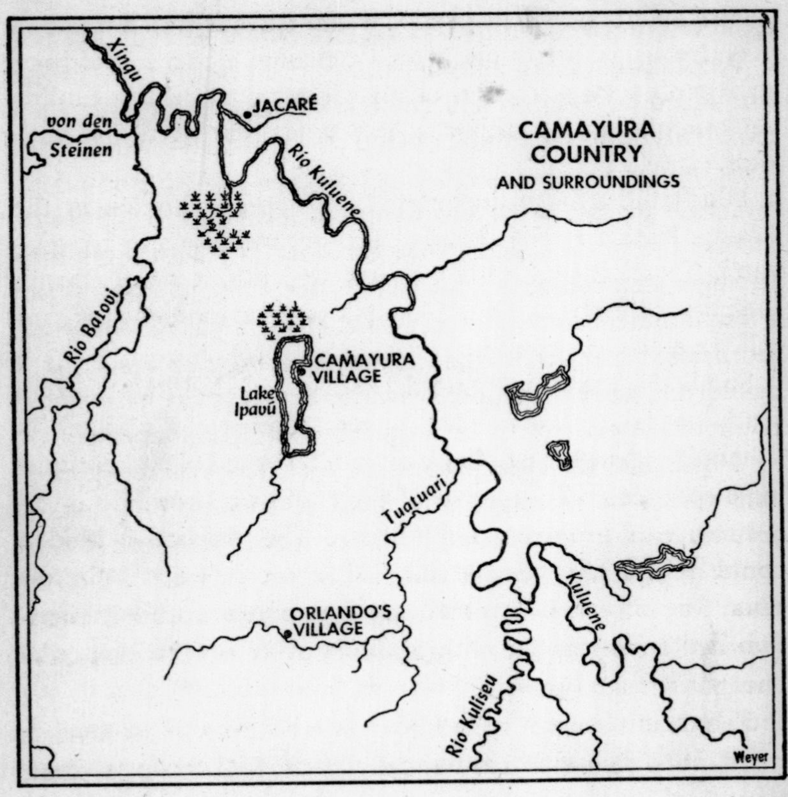

brought them here and dropped them into the lake. I feel quite humble when I think of the journey de Winton made.

He was a courageous man. He traveled a dangerous route into this country clear from the south in search of Colonel Fawcett and dropped out of sight. I have tried to locate his relatives but without success. Perhaps someone who reads this account may know of his people, who may not be aware of exactly what happened. It seems that he was murdered because he kept asking the Indians what had happened to Colonel Fawcett. They began to fear that he had come to pay back the explorer's murder, and they killed him before he could do so.*

Weeks later, in still another village, I sat next to the Indian who killed de Winton and saw the Winchester he stole from him. This Indian had just arrived in the encampment where I was, and strangely enough I had stopped myself from taking a motion picture of him as he came down the trail, because even at a distance I did not like his looks. It was the only time I remember withholding my camera for such a reason. When a few minutes later I was informed that he was de Winton's murderer, I had no desire to take a close-up. For one thing, I would not want to expose to white man's law a man whose crime ought perhaps to be judged by different standards.

When I felt the chief patting my back, I was quite surprised and was eager to return any show of friendship. I twisted around, smiling, and patted him. For lack of a tongue that he could understand, I spoke out in English, saying, "I feel the same way about you," and I could not have meant it more. He was looking at me with a kindly expression, which quite changed his appearance.

The chief's sudden friendship made a strong impression on me. I puzzled over it time and again, groping for an explanation. My attention all during this time never wandered far from my jungle brothers. Not only was I absorbed in the actions of so interesting a group of people, but my safety might depend upon knowing how they felt about me. The chief had showed no tendency earlier to "loosen up." His face wore a serious expression and his manner was distant. In fact,

*Kalervo Oberg, to whose admirable monograph entitled *Indian Tribes of Northern Mato Grosso* the reader is referred for further information on the natives of this area, gives the name of this unfortunate explorer as Thomas Winton. Harry Wright, on the other hand, who has written extensively on the Fawcett mystery, calls him Professor Albert Winter. But it is hard to question the spelling of the Brazilian writer Edmar Morél, who reports having found visiting cards left by Albert de Winton at stopping places earlier on his route.

I had begun to worry that he might not be happy over my coming. Then the change came. What caused him to show his friendly feeling is only a guess. We were passing over the spot where the bones of the other white man had been dropped into the lake. Perhaps he was putting my mind at rest by showing that, although they had killed one white man, they were not going to do the same to me.

In the direction we were paddling, I could see no sign of a village, and the farther shore looked at least three miles away. The afternoon sun was dazzling, and we kept close inshore. On the platform at the bow of our dugout stood an Indian like a bronze statue, with bow and arrow poised for fish. Brightly colored birds darted among the trees, and there was a leafy odor in the air. The workaday routine of civilized life had dropped away, and we had entered an era far from everything with which I was familiar. It was as though I had been whisked back into a world of 10,000 years ago—a reconditioned spirit on vacation from Today.

Presently there was a sound of cheerful voices and the splashing of swimmers. We rounded a point and were suddenly among a sizable group of Indians, swimming in the lake. Neither the men, women, nor children wore any clothing, either in the water or out of it. The men were uniformly lithe and muscular. There was not a thin or a fat person among them. Some of the women, with their long hair down their backs, were beautiful. There was not a trace of body hair on anyone, and their skin had the soft luster of satin.

At sight of our canoe their voices went quiet, and I could see their eyes turn in puzzlement to the white visitor. Several swam toward us to convoy our dugout to a crude dock of palm logs.

CHAPTER XIV

GOOD-BYE TO TODAY

When we reached that village on the east shore of the lake that the Camayurás called Ipavú (Ee-pah-*voo*), the sight of those clean, healthy, happy Indians made my spirits rise. This was the first time on my trip that I felt that the journey would be worth all the effort even if I were to get no farther.

I climbed out of the dugout after the chief's son, up onto the dock of palm logs.

"These are my family," he told me in Portuguese, leading me to an older woman, a brother, and two sisters.

We patted each other, smiling. These Indians had seen outsiders elsewhere, but they told me a second time that I was the first white man to visit this village. They pointed across the lake to the other village, and they also spoke of a third and a fourth, now empty I gathered, farther south around this side of the lake.

A hundred yards up from the water's edge I could see the tops of the thatched huts, set in an oval around the clearing. The men were carrying my goods up the path, and I followed. Here other Indians came forward, and I made the rounds, patting and being patted. They all had thick black hair. No one in the village was either bald or gray. Some of the women felt the light-colored hair on the back of my forearm and drew the attention of others to it.

Tah-koo-mah said, "Let me take your hammock," and he disappeared with it into the central hut.

There were nine of these huts, five of which were oval and four rectangular, as well as several open shelters for shade. Tah-koo-mah had told me that there were thirty-five people in his village, but I counted sixty at one time, and there may easily have been seventy or more. The villages of the Camayurás are semipermanent because the soil grows weak and they have to move and clear new land.

I continued to pay my respects and then, in the tradition of the Explorers Club, set my camera on its tripod to take a photograph of the club's flag in front of the hut, using the automatic shutter release. All of the flags of the Explorers Club are numbered. This was Number 16, the same that had been with the Stoll-McCracken Expedition, which I accompanied to the Arctic in 1928. The photographing of the flag baffled the Indians. They examined the flag with great curiosity and obviously wondered what on earth I was doing.

Soon Tah-koo-mah came out and said that I could take my stuff into the hut. This was the central hut but not the largest in the village. Like the others, it had a front door and a back door. Inside, bows and arrows in great number were leaning against the walls. On racks overhead near the thatching of the roof were baskets. Some ears of corn hung from the ridgepole. There were about seven hammocks.

Tah-koo-mah had strung my hammock between those of two of his sisters. One was married and was nursing a small baby. The other was unmarried and was an unusually beautiful Indian. Her name was Koo-yah-yoo. The rest were married or unmarried brothers and sisters, all fairly young. The chief never slept in this hut while I was there but used an open lean-to near by.

Koo-yah-yoo studied me shyly at first, as though to know what sort of a creature I might be. But she soon was brushing mosquitos off me as though it were a part of a hostess's duties.

As time went on, I saw that she was teasing me. She would brush unbelievable quantities of insects from my back. (I wore little here.) Then she would throw her brother a sidelong glance that said he had made quite a problem for her by bringing me. But she was always laughing before the act was over.

I piled my duffel bags under the head of my hammock and leaned my bow and arrow and canoe paddle against the wall. Two men began shouting loudly outside: *"Hooka! Hooka! Hooka!"* Hurrying to the door, I saw them circling each other in a crouching position, pawing the earth like bulls and giving out this noise. Then the two muscular figures dropped to their hands and knees and tried again and again to grab and throw each other. The struggle seemed much like our own wrestling. To win, one man had to throw the other on his back.

I set up my little Magnamite tape recorder in front of the huts, and the people of the village were greatly interested in the voices of the wild Chavantes and other sounds that I had recorded. They nearly tore the wires out in their competition to get at the headphones, and they would have worn the batteries down if I had let them. Each set of batteries was good for 100 hours of recording or playing back. I had one extra set.

Soon I could tell that they were ready to record their own talk and songs. That wonderful instrument gave me entree among strange people wherever I went.

I handed the microphone to one of the men and motioned that the sound he would put in would come back out through the headphones. He looked at it doubtfully a moment, then went into his speech just like a seasoned politician. He was a fierce fighter, who had killed two men in close combat. He grew more excited as he talked, but I could only understand two words: "Camayurá" (the name of the tribe) and

"Caraiba" (their word for white man). It didn't sound exactly as though he were turning over the keys of the city to me, and I wondered whether he was saying I would be expected to take the loyalty oath and fight for the tribe in case of attack. Almost the entire village had gathered to hear this speech, and they sat on the ground solemnly, glancing now and then, somewhat dubiously I thought, in my direction.

Then an elderly woman took the microphone. She spoke shrilly in an argumentative tone. The audience gave "the opposition" the same amount of time on the air. Her defiant pauses made it sound as though she were saying, "See, you can't answer!"

Of course everybody had to hear a sample of it through the earphones, especially the speakers themselves. Some of the women were now offering me tidbits—a delicious white sweet potato or a piece of cooked fish sandwiched between a folded piece of specially prepared pancake. This was clearly a ritual of hospitality.

Colonel Fawcett, who was killed perhaps forty miles southeast of here, had offended the Indians by refusing to eat with them in their huts. I was anxious not to appear choosy about their foods, so I accepted their gifts and returned the courtesy by making up a sugary fruit drink from dried materials I had. They would have drunk gallons if I had had the makings. However, I wanted my trade goods to go as far as possible for the collection I was to make for the American Museum. I planned therefore to depend chiefly upon my own dehydrated foods and not become indebted to them by consuming their provisions.

Some of the men went out to fish, and I took the chance to set up my cooking stove in the hut and prepare an envelope of dehydrated soup as my evening meal. Koo-yah-yoo, sitting in the hammock next to mine, watched every move. My tiny

An Indian of the Upper Xingu bathing his young daughter.

A Camayurá Indian shooting fish from the bow of the boat on the way to the village on Lake Ipavú.

The dock of palm logs from which the Camayurás bathed daily in Lake Ipavú.

The author (photographed with automatic shutter release) holding up Flag No. 16 of the Explorers Club in front of the hut in which he lived at the Camayurá village on Lake Ipavú.

Wrestling is one of the most popular sports of the Upper Xingu, and the intertribal champion is highly honored.

Nighttime revelries in the heart of Camayurá country.

Camayurás with whom the autho traveled on his expedition nea the geographical center of Sout America.

Performing what appeared to be a productivity dance. The postures of the leaf-covered arms suggest the bird dances among some of the North American Indians, but the dancer here represents a tree. The skirt is of palm fibre, the headdress gaudy with yellow and blue feathers.

Young men of the Camayurá tribe, at the raised log in the village clearing where important tribal discussions were held.

In this dance with gigantic flutes, the men made the rounds of the village, in and out of each hut.

The Camayurás also played various other sizes of flutes, down to panpipes as shown here. The panpipes seem to indicate an ancient relationship between the Amazon region and the islands of the western Pacific. Xingu tribes, lacking knives, cut hair with fish tooth set in wooden handle.

Making a dugout. The chief (standing in the boat) shaped the log with care and endless patience. The dugout was big enough to carry his family and most of his in-laws on long journeys.

Feather headdress and ear plugs, necklace of shells, red and yellow feather arm bands, and waist wrappings of native-grown cotton form the dress-up costume of the young Camayurá brave. Blue beads traded from the author encircle the man's waist.

The author showing the natives the wonders of soap bubble blowing before opening trading relations

stove, which burned kerosene under pressure and gave much heat, took her fancy. Every time I looked at her, she seemed to be saying to herself, "If I had a fire machine like that, I bet I could make something better to eat than that mess." I told her brother that I wasn't used to cooking because, as is the custom in our land, my wife did it at home.

It was fine to be able to carry a two-week supply of dried food in only ten or fifteen pounds, but the packaging was wrong for a one-man expedition. The packages were all for four persons. I had brought plenty of tape for sealing the envelopes after using part, but this did not work, for I would either get all of the salt in one part or none of it. I ended up eating enough dried beans and banana custard for four men and then wondering what was the matter with me. I lost eighteen pounds on the expedition. The potato pancakes might have been good but the packages didn't provide anything with which to grease the pan, and I hadn't time or energy to hunt for turtle eggs, which might have given satisfactory oil. Not having been able to find "instant" coffee in Rio, I had not brought any at all. I soon learned that I didn't need coffee to keep me awake at night, the village was so noisy with social and ceremonial activity.

While I was cooking this first meal, Indians crowded around to stare at me. I really lost standing when I tried to make biscuits. Using one of the fires in the hut instead of the stove, I made a rough oven out of the tinfoil envelopes. Perhaps it was because I grew up in western Pennsylvania where they make steel by the openhearth method that I turned out ingots instead of biscuits. Since my food was limited, I ate as many of the biscuits as I could. It proved only one thing—that it is not in these Indians to make fun of a visitor. Perhaps the Camayurás still think that the white man prefers his bread burned.

The two-foot pancakes of manioc that Koo-yah-yoo made were delicious. First she ground the manioc in a large wooden mortar just outside the back door of our hut. Then she unrolled a split bamboo matting about thirty inches square, which was made like an old-fashioned porch screen. She sifted the flour through this and threw away the fibrous remains. Adding water, she made a paste and spread it evenly on a two-foot pottery griddle that was held above the fire on stones. She fanned the fire from time to time with a woven-straw fire fan. When the pancake was turning yellow on the bottom, she turned it over by means of a thin wooden turner. The result was flabby and semielastic, somewhat like tripe, and chewing it suggested eating a thin rubber sponge. But it had a fascinating flavor.

The greatest hardship to endure while living with these people was their curiosity. I had come to find out how they lived, and I should not have objected to a little of my own medicine. But it really got me. At first, their curiosity was welcome. It showed friendliness. But after being watched hour after hour and day after day, it became a burden. Even when I lay in my hammock with eyes closed, I knew they were watching me. If I bent over to tie my shoestring, I would hit five of them when I straightened up. Once when I laughed, a man put his hand into my mouth to feel some gold in my teeth. The worst thing about studying another kind of people is that they study you. I was outnumbered here about 70 to 1. I've heard that freaks in the sideshow sometimes go crazy from having people look at them, and I was beginning to understand how it could be. It was fortunate that the worst of this curiosity wore off after a few days and that they began to take me for granted.

I was finishing my only meal of the day when the men burst into the hut and dropped a great heap of fish on the earth. The fish were about a foot long and three-sided in cross section. The men laid some of them in the embers of the fires and put others into large pottery bowls outside for boiling.

The kinds of fishes in the lakes and rivers of this region are too numerous to name. The most notorious are the piranhas, which are avoided by bathers, owing to their vicious habits. James Atz of the New York Zoological Society concludes that the piranha has killed more persons than any other kind of fish, including sharks and barracudas.* Professor George S. Myers of Stanford University describes it as ". . . a fish afraid of nothing, which attacks any animal, whatever its size, like lightning! [It] never attacks singly but always in schools of a hundred or a thousand! . . . a fish which, when it smells blood, turns into a raging demon."†

These fish can strip the body of an animal down to the bones in a very short time. Before swimming in a new place, I always asked the Indians whether there were any piranhas. Though we sometimes ate them, they never ate us. Of twenty related kinds, four are proved man-eaters. The Indians said, incidentally, that there were sting rays one could step on in Lake Ipavú, but that they came to the shallows to feed chiefly after sundown.

A little boy with a long pole brought a macaw in from its daytime perch in a tree and put it on a crosspiece near the roof of the hut. Night fell soon after. Outside, some of the men were shouting and chanting around a fire in the center of the clearing. Inside the thatched hut, most of the hammocks had Indians in them, and fires were burning between each two tiers to drive out the chill.

I was using the jungle hammock I had brought from New

* "Most Dangerous to Man," by James W. Atz, *Animal Kingdom*, May–June, 1954, Vol. LVIII, No. 3, pp. 75-79.

† From *Aquarium Journal*, 20: 52-61-76-85, 1949.

York, but I was soon to get a more comfortable one that the Indians made for me. The one I had was equipped with mosquito netting and could be used outdoors in the rain because there was a waterproof roof. Tah-koo-mah had made three arrow shafts of uba cane into spreaders to hold the top out. But inside the hut my civilized hammock was not as comfortable as the one the natives made. I was told, incidentally, that these huts not infrequently catch fire and burn down. So when shutting yourself up in the regulation jungle hammock with a zipper, it is wise to make sure that you don't jam the zipper and get caught inside.

That was one reason why I always put my hunting knife inside my hammock before climbing in. Also, I felt more comfortable at first with my only weapon close at hand. In darker days a number of white men lost their lives in this region. In addition to the Fawcetts, father and son, and Raleigh Rimell and Albert de Winton, a group of sixteen more recently, including five Americans, were wiped out by the Suyás not far north of here. I saw the batteries from their radio, which had been found on the beach. And there have been others. That first night at Ipavú I also took my pocketbook from my pocket and slept on it. It held all my get-home money. But when I imagined how dearly I would make anyone pay for what he tried to take, I now know I was not thinking straight. I had spent weeks buying the kind of trade goods that would be most wanted by these people—fishing line, hooks, bead necklaces, combs, mirrors, and many other articles. These things were piled loosely against the wall of the hut for any prowler to take; while I slept bravely guarding some paper money that wouldn't buy anything.

I am now sure that it made a great difference that I had been invited to visit this village. As every explorer knows, the native does not usually steal from his own people but rather from an enemy tribe or from a stranger. Without going into all the little ways in which the visitor can preserve his welcome among a people different from himself, I can say with certainty that his position as a guest is his most valuable insurance. A friend of mine has on his coat of arms the motto: "All countries are homeland to a brave man." Courage draws admiration wherever we see it. Yet I believe I would put more faith in the motto: "All countries are homeland to a sympathetic man," expecially if with sympathy is linked an understanding of local courtesies.

Before putting my pocketbook under me in my hammock, I saw in it a lone coin—the one I hadn't dropped into the subway turnstile at Times Square that last day in New York when I took a taxi instead. In a strange way that little symbol of civilization made me know more sharply than anything else how far I had come. I never felt farther from home in my life. Entering the life of people like these is like having the switch pulled. The scene in the hut, lighted dimly by fires, might have been in prehistoric times. The Indians were talking and laughing in their hammocks. The mothers were swinging gently with their babies. Now and then, one would warm her child by blowing her breath on it through her closed teeth with a hissing sound. This was one of the typical night noises in the hut. No one wore any clothing. Some of the Indians had dozed off, and once in a while I would hear someone talking in his sleep.

I found a strong beauty in this jungle hut, with its hammocks and people and timeless tools of living. I have rarely felt more at peace than I did there on the shores of Lake Ipavú, where people I was beginning to admire greatly thought I had gone to sleep and had stopped watching me.

CHAPTER XV

A DAY BEFORE YESTERDAY

It was barely light when I woke up to see Koo-yah-yoo in the doorway of our hut pouring water over herself from a gourd. She was tall for her tribe—perhaps five feet six inches, which is above the average for the men. Her movements were always graceful, whether she was combing her hair with a nicely made bamboo comb or twisting cord with the palm of her hand against her thigh. In the distance, I could hear the voices of others swimming in the lake. Presently the young men came streaming in, dripping and glistening. Every morning their musical screams sounded through the village as they came running from the lake. They were full of animal spirits.

The new day was typical of all that followed. After bathing in the lake, I swam out to deep water, filled my canvas bucket, and brought it in for boiling. On the rivers, when at least twenty or thirty miles downstream from the nearest Indian village, I drank the water without worry, but here at the lake I didn't want to take chances. I even boiled the water for brushing my teeth.

Though this place is only 12 degrees from the equator, it was quite cold in the early morning, around 55°. Without fires in the hut, sleep would have been impossible. The Indians make no cloth and they go from birth to death with no protection, except during certain ceremonies when they wear a "grass skirt." Neither the men nor the women showed any hesitation about urinating in front of others. They went some distance from the village to relieve their bowels, but I don't think they did so to escape notice. Of course, the babies had nothing in the way of diapers, and you had to be careful when standing near a woman holding one because it might sprinkle you. More than once, Tah-koo-mah's sister, having been fouled by her infant, asked me for paper instead of leaves, which she would ordinarily have used. But they kept themselves clean by bathing frequently.

The small three-sided "fig leaf" (*uluri*) that all the women of the upper Xingu wear is a curious item. It is no larger than one of those triangular Cape of Good Hope postage stamps and is made from the inner bark of a tree. A thin fiber string from its lower point goes down between the legs and up to the base of the spine. One of the supposedly authoritative books says that they tie this string to the waist cord at the back, but they did not where I was. They let it stick out about an inch behind. Also, I have heard it erroneously said that the women are as ashamed without this tiny protection as we would be completely naked, but this is not true. They left the *uluri* off about a third of the time and didn't care if I saw them without it. I wore no clothes a good bit of the time, and neither the men, women, nor children showed any interest.

Childbirth in a village like this can occur in full view of the children, and arouses no particular attention. I have no doubt that the Indians might perform their marriage activities in sight of others, though I never saw them do so. When a man of the tribe suggested that one of the girls would not object if I took her in the direction of some shade shelters at the farther end of the village, I wondered whether this was a special place. I had felt that I was less welcome in that direction, but it may have been my imagination or just coincidence. However, there could be no doubt about what the man meant. According to Kalervo Oberg, they would bury a "fatherless child" alive.

Contrary to the reports that come to us from some other parts of the world where people live in a primitive state, the Camayurás knew what makes a woman pregnant. The knowledge may be quite old with them, for they use the same word for "semen" as for "son."

These Indians had never had contact with missionaries, but one husband to one wife was the usual rule among them, and I got the impression in various intangible ways that "respectable" married life was wanted here. To be a member of a well-regulated family was a source of pride, and the parent-child relationship was one of respect on both sides. The older members of the tribe clearly expected and received obedience. There was no evidence of the sexual looseness that some persons of narrow upbringing might expect among people who went around without any clothes on. I didn't hear of anything approaching the "ceremonial promiscuity" of the Eskimos, in which on special occasions the lights are put out and the usual marriage ties are laid aside. The Camayurás doubtless have a less moralistic attitude about marital fidelity than we do. To understand how the people in a primitive group of this sort look upon marriage, one has to realize how important the economic ties are that result from the division of labor between the husband and the wife. Yet I think that if unfaithfulness were frequent, the offended spouse would show it, and I didn't see any scolding while I was here. However, I did hear later that Tah-koo-mah's father, the chief, had given one of his daughters in marriage but had sent the man away when he proved unable to keep her for himself. The girl then married another man and took a fresh start.

A young man in the Camayurá tribe usually goes to live in the hut of his wife's father and works for him for perhaps a year after marriage. The son-in-law has to show great respect toward his wife's father. As for his mother-in-law, he is not even supposed to speak directly to her but only through his wife or someone else. More than one family lived in these large thatched huts, usually several related families such as brothers and their wives. The Camayurás prefer to marry their first cousins. A man marries the daughter of his father's sister or of his mother's brother. This so-called cross-cousin marriage is a widespread custom among primitive people. With us, there is a superstition that the children of first cousins will be deaf mutes. When Charles Darwin's son, Sir George Howard Darwin, fell in love with his first cousin, he made an intensive statistical study of cousin marriages to find out whether they produced deaf mutes, and he found conclusively that they didn't. That was almost a century ago, but the superstition still lingers. Among the Camayurás, first cousins were *expected* to marry each other.

I was sorry that a wedding did not occur while I was in this village. Kalervo Oberg reports that the young couples of this tribe are recognized as married when they cut each other's hair after coming out of seclusion at the end of the puberty period. This all happens at the time of an important yearly ceremony known as the Kwarúp, at which time the people also honor those who have died during the year. It is their custom to bury the dead in the central clearing of the last village they lived in. An important chief has a little room dug out underground for him, in which his body lies in his hammock held between two posts.

A woman brought me a sick child, and that started it. When I had taken its temperature and given it some aspirin, four other children were brought to me with temperatures that ranged from 101.5 to 105.6 degrees with the thermometer under the arm. I was afraid that the 105.6-degree baby was almost dead. Her eyes were glued shut with infection.

I am not a medical doctor, but I had a lot of good drugs. I tried to tell the Indians how ill this child was, because I didn't want to be blamed for her death. It is easy to get in wrong with the medicine man. The mother only stared at me like a frightened animal, but when I measured the antibiotic powder and asked for some water, she produced instead some of her breast milk. We mixed it with the medicine in a gourd spoon Tah-koo-mah had brought and fed it to the baby. I examined my patients every four hours.

From noon to three o'clock was the hard part of the day for me because of the heat. I slept some, which was easy because the nighttime revelries around the campfire had kept me awake late.

The men and women worked separately at their jobs. While the wife was processing manioc, the husband might be making a bow or an arrow, some distance off. The women usually sat right on the ground while they worked. The men sometimes sat on a low stool carved out of a single piece of wood in the shape of a bird or an animal.

Manioc is the poisonous relative of our tapioca plant. One of the mysteries of anthropology is how the Indians discovered that a poisonous plant could be made edible by a process that is not simple. How could the person who ate it and got sick know that he had discovered a valuable food? It contains prussic acid, a strong poison, and anyone who ate it would have to work fast to discover how to "cure" the root or himself before he died.

The women were busy with the processing of manioc the entire time I was there. Sometimes they even worked by moonlight. One woman would be scraping the two-foot roots with a shell and washing them. Another would take them from her and grate them on a board set with hundreds of nail-like thorns from the tucum palm tree. The grater was laid across a huge pottery bowl, which sometimes was almost three feet across. The grated pulp fell into the bowl, where it was mixed with cold water. A third woman, working over a bowl of her own, would squeeze the washed pulp by rolling it up in a thin bamboo matting. This procedure sounds easy, but each step took time, and without it the roots would still contain the poison.

The men were making large leaf-lined baskets in which to store the processed manioc. These were not woven or plaited as baskets usually are. They were made by forming a box-shaped frame of four oval hoops of vines and two circular ones for the ends, forming a framework about a yard long. The space inside the hoops was filled in with an open network of lashing. The basket was lined with green leaves. A man could make one of these in about an hour if the materials were at hand.

Greater nicety was shown in the making of arrows, which were real works of art. Most of them were over five feet long. The Indians would lash the foreshaft neatly into the shaft and make the lashings waterproof by twirling them against a piece of heated resin. The point was usually the spine of a sting ray or the curved rib of an animal, sharpened at both ends and lashed to the foreshaft so that the hind point stuck out as a barb to keep the arrow from coming out of the wound.

The type of arrow that made a loud whistling sound in flight had a blunt head made of a hollowed tucum palm nut with slots cut in it. It was said that the sound would hold a bird motionless so that the arrow would hit it and stun it. I often saw and heard the Indians using this arrow for practice or fun but never tested its hypnotic effect on birds.

One of the most surprising weapons was in the hand of

an Indian I met once while walking a trail alone. He and his wife suddenly came into view quite naked in front of me on the upper Tuatuarí River. She was very shy, and he was a bit uncertain of me. Since his manner was hardly casual, I stepped off the trail and waved him past as though to say, "This is your forest, not mine." He hesitated, as though afraid. Then I tried to tell him I had been at Lake Ipavú and knew Chief Kutamapú and others. He immediately relaxed and showed me his spear. It was formed of two pieces that fitted together to make a shaft 22 feet long! I gathered from his motions that it was for spearing fish at the bottom of clear rivers.

My friends at Lake Ipavú made the best bows in the region, huge ones about seven feet long with good striking power. Other friendly tribes traded for them with the Camayurás.

It was pleasant to watch their fingers moving skillfully at work so different from any we see. Usually they didn't object to my nosing around. It is their nature to come right out with their feelings, and sometimes I would feel someone patting me on the back. But once I must have pushed my welcome too far. I was taking pictures of the women preparing food when one girl began angrily throwing gobs of wet manioc at me. One gob gummed up my camera badly. My first impulse was to withdraw and reconsider my position. But I had made it a rule never to let an Indian stay angry for more than sixty seconds, if I could help it. Once a native has "gone on record" that he is angry, it creates a much worse problem. So I leapt back into the battle, taking imaginary manioc out of my eyes and ears and giving the girl to believe that she had ruined my camera. The second hand worked around toward the finish mark; then she began to grin, and so did her companions.

A little later in the day I went off into the forest with some of the men to see where they were making a dugout. About a quarter of a mile from the village we threaded our way through the rough clearing where they grew their manioc and other plants. The cultivated field was a winding, irregular tangle of stumps, half-burned trees, and scraggly growth. I noticed some cotton plants here. Evidently the Camayurás have for many centuries grown enough cotton for the cross strings in their hammocks (the lengthwise ones being of palm fibre) and for the heavy wrappings that they sometimes wind around their arms, legs, or waist.

The heat was still extreme, but in the narrow clearing where the dugout was being made the glare of the sun was cut off. The chief took quiet pride in the boat that was taking shape under his hands, and well he might because he did a beautiful job and worked harder than all the rest put together. I grew to admire the wisdom and dignity with which Kutamapú used his authority. He had no badge of office. He was not the warrior type and did not owe his power to force. He had the welfare of his people at heart and looked farther ahead than the rest. Like Joshua the son of Nun, he never stopped till the work was done. He kept chipping away lovingly on the log, using a strange curved blade that had been traded from I know not where. It was one of the few metal tools I saw in the village. There is some question whether the Camayurás may not have learned how to make dugouts in fairly recent times from the Juruna tribe to the north. In making their commoner canoe, which is of bark, a scaffold is built around a jatobá tree and wedges are used to pry off the bark. It is then shaped while soft. The front is bent up flat, but a sort of accordion pleat is made in the stern so that the back edge has the shape of a W. They fill the W with mud because a certain amount of water would otherwise come in.

Back in the clearing, I made my evening meal at 4:30 and then examined my patients. Some were improving; some seemed the same. Around 7:00 I made an unwanted discovery.

Each night about this time, as it turned out, the men gathered around the fire and smoked ten-inch cigars about the size of lead pencils. In making these, the Camayurás seemed to wrap tobacco in leaves of several other kinds, and perhaps there is something in these leaves to affect more than the taste. For I noticed that Tah-koo-mah, after smoking awhile, lost his Portuguese tongue for the rest of the evening and talked gibble-gabble. Since he was the only person here with whom I could communicate, this was inconvenient.

I wondered what might be in the cigars and whether smoking one of them would help me to understand more. I tried this, but it only made me care less. Perhaps Tah-koo-mah was simply entering into the ceremonial spirit, which had a strong hold on the men each evening. The women never smoked but sometimes joined the men and sang songs of their own. This tribe had no alcoholic drinks.

When I could do so without risk of giving the impression I was trying to buy the chief's daughter, I gave Kutamapú a magnificent large knife that had served me well. It was one of the finest presents I had brought, and the chief prized it. But there was something almost ceremonial in the way he passed it over to the others, as though to show it was for the use of the tribe.

The noises of the night were memorable. Wanting to record the sounds around the clock, I had brought along an alarm watch. But I didn't need it to wake me. The trouble was in getting to sleep before daybreak. Much of the night the men shouted, sang, caterwauled, imitated animals and birds, and filled in with forced laughter. In the tropics in a jungle village like this, it gets dark right after sundown, and there isn't any light except from the campfires. It is too dark to play games, and there is no place to go. The Indians can't visit amusement centers or read or listen to the radio. They can't sleep the whole night; it is too long. So sound effects have come to play a big part in their night life. I think the Indians also like to make a noise to discourage raids from enemy tribes, which are sometimes carried out in order to capture women or right a wrong. Tah-koo-mah's own mother, as a matter of fact, had been captured by the Camayurás from the Suyás, a dangerous tribe to the north.

Sometimes they sang, sometimes they played their flutes, and sometimes they just shouted. I tried to discover the signal that touched off a certain yell they had. All of a sudden, after a moment of silence, six or eight of the men would break into a yell that went up the scale, hesitated a moment, then began a little higher and came back down. It ended in wholehearted but completely joyless laughter. They sometimes did this in the daytime as well as at night.

I was lying in my hammock one night trying to sleep when I got quite a start. In the flickering firelight I couldn't see much and was just dozing off when a devil-dancer wearing a mask came in. Sometimes three spooks together would rush into the hut, perhaps specially for my benefit. After frightening everyone back against the walls, they would go out. Once an Indian apparently impersonating a blind old man was led in by a young boy. He was looking for something or somebody, and his falsetto voice made him sound like a spirit from the other world.

I spent much of the night sitting on the men's log by the fire in the clearing, but when I went to my hammock to record my diary on the tape recorder, I left a second microphone out in the clearing in case I heard sounds worth recording.

Around 3:30 on this particular night, I was lying in my hammock when the racket gave way to haunting flute music. Its quality made me sure that the sickest child I had been treating was dying and that the Indians were trying to hold its spirit on earth. So I pulled myself out of my hammock and went to the hut. I was not at all sure I was giving the right medicine and feared that the situation might be touchy. These large oval huts have two poles that run up to the roof like the poles in a circus tent. The hammocks are strung from the poles out to the wall in all directions like the spokes of a wheel. There isn't just one layer of hammocks but two or even three. The result is that in the dark it is difficult to get from one part of the hut to another. You have to pick your way over some hammocks and under others. In order to know my sick children, I had drawn a small plan of the village and numbered the places where they slept. I knew where to find this little girl, but it was something else to get there in the dark. Halfway through the hammocks, I lost my balance and fell across the body of a sleeping Indian and nearly startled him out of his senses. From the noise he let out, he must have thought the Chavantes were attacking.

I found the mother lying in her hammock with the baby girl. Her fever was about the same, but she was still living, and I gave her another dose. Tah-koo-mah later denied that the flute music had been for the sick girl and said that it was for something to do with the sky. This, however, may have been another way of saying the same thing.

By now, others were roused, and I had to visit all my patients. It was chilly at this hour, and when I got back to my hut I was glad that Koo-yah-yoo had blown the fire until it was crackling brightly. I thanked her with gestures for its warmth, and I'm sure that she knew what I meant. She must have thought me quite a curiosity. It would be easy to imagine that she was thinking, as I was, about the great gulf of time and space that separated her world from mine, but actually she knew nothing of history or the great round earth as we think of it. When I told her, through her brother, that it took an airplane thirty hours, flying as fast as it could, to come from where I lived, she showed great wonderment. I tried to tell her what lay between—forests and mountains and water too wide to see across—but I don't think she could picture it. Brought up to know only a few miles of lakes and rivers, Koo-yah-yoo could probably visualize with greater realism the myths of her tribe, which say that the Creator, Mavutsiné, married a wooden woman and produced the sun and the moon. To Koo-yah-yoo, the airplanes that sometimes fly over this wilderness are the spirit of the mythical hawk, Apacaní, who was captured by a legendary tribal ancestor and as a result sent death to the world. And I, as a white man, would have descended from a pair of women also created by Mavutsiné. If you are imagining that she looked upon me as some sort of a god, I must deny it. Nor had I any wish to set myself up as something special, though it might have been easy to do so with a few tricks picked up at any joke store. I was more interested in watching these people act as if no stranger were around.

In the other end of the hut, the cold had awakened a baby in the hammock with its mother, and it was whimpering. The mother strengthened her own fire and warmed the child by blowing her breath on him. Outside in the moonlight, the fire had gone out under a huge manioc pot. It would be relighted in the morning from embers. The Indians never had to make fire while I was here. They kept it going, but if need be they could kindle it by twirling a stick in a piece of wood between their palms.

The flute music had died down now, and the night was silent except for the noises of insects and the unending patter of the dogs' feet. They seemed to have a running game all their own after the world had gone to sleep.

CHAPTER XVI

EDEN OR BACKWASH

Within twenty-four hours the temperature of the sickest child was normal, and her mother had bathed and fed her. The most obstinate of my little invalids, though not by any means the sickest, still registered 101.5 degrees. His mother kept his body daubed with spots of resin about as big as quarters, probably for some ceremonial or curative purpose. He was about seven or eight months old. He, too, seemed to be improving toward the end of my visit, with treatments for dysentery and malaria.

My "miracle drugs" aroused only a quiet gratitude in the mothers. Something else, to my surprise, brought a far warmer response. I had been in the village several days before I thought to say how much I liked it here.

"Your village is one of the prettiest places I have ever seen," I told Tah-koo-mah, "and I like your people very much!"

He could not conceal his pleasure. And when he thought I wasn't looking, I saw him tell the others.

A new friendliness came into their manner. He alone had been responsible for my coming here, and it was just as if my roommate in college had asked me home for the holidays. He wanted me to like his people, and he was anxious to have them like me.

Expecially when the sun was setting across the lake, with all the clouds aflame, the village at Ipavú had the tropical beauty that we think of in the South Seas. Because of its simplicity and innocence, I thought of it as a sort of Garden of Eden. The Indians did not attach evil to the unclothed body. They had not learned the trick of thinking one thing and saying another.

In all the world it would be hard to find a people whose unspoiled simplicity gave a better chance to see whether the "Noble Savage" described by the French philosopher Jean Jacques Rousseau was real or imaginary. When, in 1749, Rousseau portrayed primitive man as the only perfect person and condemned civilization as having destroyed everything good in human nature, he became famous almost overnight. It was in the period before the French and American Revolutions. Many had begun to doubt that the nobility were noble; they were ready to see virtue in the lowliest of God's creatures. Amid the crowded living conditions of the cities, with their frightful epidemics, it was easy to imagine that in the great outdoors, especially in the abundance of tropical nature, man still had the happiness that was his original birthright. Rousseau argued that primitive man had lived in a perfect state of innocence as long as he had been a creature of nature; it was only when he fell under the degrading influences of civilization that he became sinful. This interpretation was opposite to the conventional religious doctrine of original sin, which holds that the fall of man occurred at the very start in the Garden of Eden, while life was yet simple.

The idea of the Noble Savage and his original innocence has colored our thoughts right up to the present. Romantic writers, who may never have had to light a fire with wet wood, portrayed our own Indians as we wanted to see them, without troubling to check against the facts. And the artists who drew pictures of them added a classic touch by giving them the bodies of Greek gods and goddesses.

Today we try not to invent facts to fit our theories. Our aim is to study the facts and discover what they prove. We want to know what different environments do to people. We also seek to learn how different social and spiritual outlooks affect people's ability to adjust to life's conditions. Unfortunately, it is almost too late to learn from primitive man, because the last of the truly uncivilized natives are nearly gone. Just when the techniques of anthropology and psychology have reached a useful stage, with portable sound recording, rapid action cameras, and improved methods of analyzing facts and acts and thoughts, we find ourselves almost without any primitive people to try them out on. Some of the last of them are here in the southern part of the Amazon Basin.

It is easy to idealize the life of the man of nature. Many things in his customs are apt to confuse us at first. Away from the complexities of civilization, we do not see the familiar problems, or at least do not recognize them, and we need to guard against imagining that the people have no special troubles of their own. Actually, the native of the wilderness may be plagued by taboos, shortage of vital materials, the fear of blood vengeance, or the threats of the witch doctor. The Noble Savage is neither noble nor savage in the generally accepted sense, so far as I have seen him. He is generally a good fellow, much more like yourself than the movies would lead you to believe, with the same weaknesses and the same inclination to exploit an advantage. Within the framework of his customs, he has the same capacity for heroism.

The code of the Camayurá derives much of its character from the size of the "in-group"—the group within which all co-operate for the common good and regard each other as bound together by love or loyalty. Among these people social responsibility was limited much more to the family and village. They were not a warlike people, but it was honorable to kill an enemy tribesman a few miles away just as with us a man is made a hero for downing an enemy plane somewhere on the other side of the world. The Camayurá, besides lacking anything like our national allegiance, is without the many other overlapping and sometimes conflicting group responsibilities familiar to us in our political party, church, civic council, service club, trade union, or fraternal organization. So his social adjustments are simple, and, seeing them, we are impressed with how complex ours have become.

My jungle brothers had their troubles—fear of enemy tribes, the possibility of crop failure, tropical storms to which they had to expose their bare bodies for hours at a time, perhaps rivalries within the group and other problems I could not see. But for all that, they were happy people, and I have seen many Indians who weren't. They were full of good humor and approached life on the positive side. Their code, though strict in its way, involved no apparent inconsistencies. Their sports and ceremonials gave them deep emotional satisfaction. The cycle of daily activities, though far less varied than ours in most respects, did not pigeonhole a man in a job of endless repetition, and they never appeared bored at their work.

But even Rousseau, with his faith in the nobleness and innocence of primitive man, did not pretend that we could return to the jungle state. Our problem, just as in his day, is to raise our social and spiritual development to a level comparable to our ability to solve technical problems.

The joy with which the Indians entered into their dances was a delight to see. The nighttime activities were emotionally more impressive, as might be expected, but the daytime dances were the most beautiful, and the Indians were quite willing to let me take pictures of them.

The dance called Tavurawá was performed to make the plants and trees grow. The men put on grass skirts and gorgeous headdresses and covered their arms with leaves to look like boughs. Plenty of the bright red *urucú* was used, and they even painted me up, so that I felt quite in the spirit of the thing. They danced to the music of a thumping gourd and a rattle, holding their arms out like wings in a way reminiscent of some of the Indian bird dances in our Southwest. Two women took part toward the end, going around behind the men, which seemed to be a common custom in dances among these people.

After the dance, I saw the chief's son looking at the sky, in which there were a few clouds to the northwest. I was surprised when he said to me: "It is going to rain soon."

"Rain!" I said. "This is the dry season. It can't possibly rain."

But Tah-koo-mah only repeated that it was going to rain.

Knowing how well people of the wilderness can sometimes tell the weather, I was ready to believe that he might be right. But I now think that they performed this dance out of season so I could see it and that Tah-koo-mah meant that the dance was sure to make it rain. To read the signs of the sky would be science, whereas to do a dance to make it rain would be to them religion, to us superstition. But it did sprinkle. It was the only rain I saw during my whole stay in Mato Grosso.

I recorded many spiritual songs on my portable tape recorder and took pictures of an interesting "spook" dance performed by a man wearing a gourd over his head the size of a Halloween pumpkin, with flaring ears of woven matting. But the most beautiful ceremony was the giant flute dance called the Uruá. Two men in ceremonial headdress and carrying flutes seven feet long danced side by side around the village, ducking into each hut in turn and performing a short dance inside. Most of the hammocks had to be taken down for this dance, and the household goods were moved against the walls. It went on for hours in the hot sun, and I couldn't learn the purpose. It looked as though the dancers might be blessing or cleansing the houses, but that is only a guess.

Toward the end of this dance, Koo-yah-yoo and another young woman joined the men, following around close behind them in perfect step, each with the right hand on the shoulder of the man in front. Unlike the men, the women only added one decorative touch to their normal nudity—a delicate "tail" made of a single curved fiber the thickness of a broom-straw. It stuck up behind about a foot and a half. The rhythm and agility of the dancers would have satisfied the requirements of a Broadway producer. The right foot marked the time throughout. The doorways to the huts were so low that one had to stoop to get in, but the dancers, with these enormous flutes, were able to duck into them one at a time so smoothly that it was like a continuous flow of color. Each flute was made up of two tubes, one seven feet long, the other five. They were of split bamboo, hollowed out and lashed together with rosin. The men held these enormous instruments with only one hand, and the team performed in perfect unison.

Smaller flutes a little over two feet long were played on other occasions, and two of them are now in the Museum's collections. This tribe also had panpipes, but they do not do much with them.

During the first dance, a small hut was constructed of boughs in the center of the clearing, and I was asked not to enter it—the only restriction during my stay with the Camayurás. In this ceremonial hut, various sacred objects were kept. I never saw the most sacred flute, which is a yard or so in length. Women especially are forbidden to see it. Kalervo Oberg says that if a woman were to see the sacred flute, she would be taken into the woods, raped by all the men, and left to die.

A lighthearted solemnity semed to possess Koo-yah-yoo and her girl friend during the flute dance. It was an exhausting exercise that went on hour after hour in the broiling sun. After it was over, Koo-yah-yoo filled a huge gourd with water at the lake and came hurrying up to the hut, light as a feather. Inside, she lifted the gourd over her head, poured water over herself, and washed her arms, legs, and body. When she rinsed off, the water began to splash me in my hammock. Her back was toward me, and I couldn't keep from reaching out and giving her little wisplike tail a tug. An electric shock could scarcely have startled her more. She jumped away, whirling around at the same time and scolding me. Her words were sharp, but they were soon over. She smiled finally, and I knew that if I had broken a tribal taboo she wasn't going to tell on me.

So it was that I was able to watch all the activities of the village at this season, with an easiness that it would be difficult ever again to win among a group of native people. Hut building, hammock weaving, string making, the making of arrows, the building of a boat, and endlessly the processing and storing of manioc—all this in a continuous round.

CHAPTER XVII

HOW DID THEY COME?

Some of the Camayurás' tools were Asiatic in origin, as would be expected among people whose ancestors came from Asia and found use for these old things down through the centuries. Whether you accept the story of the Creation as told in the Book of Genesis or the findings of evolutionary science, you will believe that the human race originated in the Old World, probably in Asia. The Indians are an offshoot of the Yellow or Mongoloid race, and their forefathers came to America by way of Bering Strait before civilization as we know it got started.

The tools and techniques of the Camayurás that were brought from Asia are old ones. I refer to such things as the bow and arrow, the spear thrower, the art of making fire by twirling a stick, the bull-roarer (a noise-making slat of wood tied to a string), strings of perforated shells and teeth, the domesticated dog, whistles, and perhaps flutes. Human history before the use of any metals is divided into three parts: Old Stone Age (Paleolithic), Middle Stone Age (Mesolithic), and New Stone Age (Neolithic). The following list shows that most of the Camayurás' Asiatic things were known in the Old Stone Age. All had been invented by the Middle Stone Age.

As recently as 1925 there was no direct evidence that human beings reached North or South America more than 3,000 or 4,000 years ago. But in 1926 and 1927 a special

Ancient Discoveries from Europe and Asia

Object	*When Invented*	*Explanation*
Bow and arrow	Surely in Middle Stone Age, probably in Old Stone Age	
Spear thrower	Magdalenian period of Old Stone Age	A specially shaped board on which the spear is laid so as to give extra leverage in throwing it
Fire stick	Presumably Old Stone Age	
Bull-roarer	Old Stone Age	A whirring piece of wood attached to a stick with cord. It has strong ceremonial meaning in many parts of the world and is commonly hidden from the women
Strings of shells and teeth	Magdalenian period of Old Stone Age	
Tame Dogs	Middle Stone Age	
Whistles and perhaps flutes	Magdalenian period of Old Stone Age	
Pottery	Magdalenian period of Old Stone Age. More important in Middle Stone Age. Plentiful in New Stone Age	Probably invented independently in the Americas
Clay figures	Magdalenian period of Old Stone Age	
Ground stone tools, as distinct from chipped or flaked ones	The beginnings of this art began in the Middle or Old Stone Age, but its application to axes came in the New Stone Age	Perhaps independently developed in the Americas

kind of flint points known as Folsom points were discovered. They were found in association with extinct animals of the Ice Age, and this pushed the date of man's arrival in the New World considerably farther back. The Carbon 14 method of determining the age of organic remains has recently proved that the Folsom people were living in the United States at least 11,000 years ago. A throwing stick, 7,038 (plus or minus 350) years old was found in Nevada. Some sandals 9,053 (plus or minus 350) years old have turned up in Oregon. Charcoal indicates that man lived in Nebraska 10,493 (plus or minus 1,500) years ago, and in Utah 11,453 (plus or minus 600) years ago. There is a date of 9,883 (plus or minus 350) years ago from Texas. There is even evidence that man reached the southern tip of South America, 8,639 (plus or minus 450) years ago. In 1954, fragments of a skull found below the Folsom level in Texas were estimated to be between 2,000 and 10,000 years older than Folsom Man.

But one date exceeds even this. In 1932, Fenley Hunter, who hunts for the remains of prehistoric animals as a hobby, was digging with Albert C. Silberling in Nevada, and they came upon a piece of volcanic glass chipped by the hand of man. It was imbedded in material that had become stonelike, and near it were the teeth and bones of a prehistoric bison, a camel, and a horse. There was also a quantity of charcoal from a prehistoric campfire. The Carbon 14 method had not been discovered then, but in 1953, when the charcoal from that campfire in Nevada was put through the test, its age was shown to be 23,800 years or more.

At the same time that the Carbon 14 method has extended the antiquity of man in North and South America, it has proved the Old Stone Age in Europe to be somewhat less ancient than was previously thought. A few years ago it was customary to assign an age of 20,000 or 25,000 years to the latter part of the Old Stone Age. The Cro-Magnon people, who painted such fine pictures of animals in the caves of southwestern Europe, were known to have lived around or after the peak of the last Ice Age. But the C-14 method has shown that the great glaciers came south for the last time only about 11,000 years ago both in Europe and North America. So, instead of assigning a ripe age of 20,000 years to these Old Stone Age people of Europe, we now know that the last of them lived no more than 11,000 years ago, at about the same time as Folsom Man in North America. However, in the earlier human types, such as Java Man and Peking Man, the Old World still claims a wide priority.

The discoveries that increase man's known antiquity in North and South America help to explain why the natives of these two continents never were heir to such important inventions of the New Stone Age as wheeled vehicles, plows, stringed musical instruments, the potter's wheel, and the raising of a large variety of domestic animals for the performance of work or the production of meat and milk. In Egypt, the New Stone Age saw the domestication of barley and wheat about 6,400 years ago. Flax, cattle, pigs, goats, and sheep were other developments. Eastern Asia produced rice, sugar cane, chickens, water buffaloes, the Asiatic pig, horses, and camels. These are the things we usually associate with the New Stone Age, but the Indians of the upper Xingu had none of them. In place of them, they had some purely American developments. The dog, known from the Middle Stone Age, was their only domestic animal, though they kept various birds as pets or for their feathers. Their basic food plant was manioc, and they grew various other American plants in smaller quantity. Other American developments include the hammock, the one-piece bark canoe, and the technique of poisoning fish with various vines. It might be well, therefore, to call their way of life the American New Stone Age, as a reminder that the things that raised them above the previous stage are quite different from the ones we are used to thinking of in connection with the New Stone Age in Asia or Europe.

Years ago, when archaeology was in its infancy, the Old Stone Age was defined as the period of chipped or flaked stone implements. People were said to have reached the New Stone Age when they developed the technique of grinding an edge on their stone axes. Today, many more important inventions and discoveries are known to have marked the New Stone Age, such as the domestication of animals and the development of agricultural techniques and tools, so that the grinding of stone blades looks rather insignificant. It was not even new in the New Stone Age except as applied to axes. People in the Middle Stone Age, and even in the Old, had been grinding edges on other tools.

One of the few Asiatic implements the Camayurás had of which I have not been able to find evidence in Asia or Europe earlier than the New Stone Age is the spindle whorl for spinning thread. This exception is interesting because the spindle whorl is used with cotton, and cotton is one of the very few crops that was raised both in Asia and South America before modern contact. The Camayurá Indians grew cotton and had the spindle for making it into thread, but they did not weave it into cloth. Whether cotton was domesticated independently in America from a plant related to the Old World cotton plant or brought from Asia to America by primitive people is not known. It seems to be a later acquisition than the other things that are definitely Asiatic. But this does not disturb the supposition that the original Asiatic ancestors of the Camayurás came to America no later than the Middle Stone Age.

Both the whistle and the arrow are probably from the Old

Stone Age, but the combination of the two in the whistling arrow cannot, so far as I know, be proved to be as old, though it may be. The Camayurás are not the only people in South America who make the whistling arrow, and it is known also from eastern Asia.

The more I saw of these fascinating folk of the forest, the more curious I became about the long dark ages through which their forefathers had struggled to reach the brief twilight in which it is our privilege to see them. In the presence of a group of Indians on the upper Xingu, or more especially among the Chavantes, one can scarcely escape the feeling that he is looking into one of the early chapters of human history. The Chavantes do not use hammocks, and I did not see them with canoes, though they may have them. Otherwise, their culture is similar to that of the Camayurás in that they both depend upon the bow and arrow and practice a simple form of farming. Both have the dog and pottery, and both live in thatched huts. Neither seems to make any use of stone points for arrows or spears; they depend instead upon sharpened bone and bamboo, the spines of fishes, and the like.

The Chavantes live in greater isolation from neighboring tribes than other Indians in this region, and their attitude toward whites as well as toward other Indians shows a limitation of outlook and a determined ignorance of the outside world. Their hostility may have increased in recent times. On the other hand, there may be something ancient in it, a traditional defiance toward the outside world that may have been passed down from father to son for a long time. We find them living inland from the rivers that other tribes have used as avenues of trade and travel. This encourages the belief that they may be the hard central core of conservatism in this part of South America and that they may bring us closer than other jungle tribes to the ancient ways.

Here we are dealing with a length of time so great that it is hard for most of us to grasp it. The Great Glacier spread down over much of North America for the last time about 11,000 years ago. Primitive man reached North America before that time, hunting prehistoric mammoths and bison. If the dating of Fenley Hunter's chipped stone from Nevada is correct (and the carbon is being put through a more refined test), the people who shaped it probably came to North America during an interglacial period. The climate at that time, even along the Bering Sea migration route, may have been quite different from today. We are still in the end of the last Ice Age and may not have yet reached the full mildness of an interglacial period. If the ancestors of our jungle Indians traveled the Bering Strait route before the last advance of the Great Glacier, their way of life might not have had to adjust to such drastic climatic changes as we are used to thinking of.

The variety of languages among the Indians of North and South America also indicates that the Indians have been in this hemisphere considerably longer than was once imagined. Eighty or more families of languages are recognized in North and South America. The Bering Strait migration route is a narrow corridor, and we can scarcely imagine that these varied tongues arrived, one after another, after having been fully developed in Asia. Language experts have scarcely found a single American Indian language that is clearly and definitely related by vocabulary as well as grammatic structure to any Asiatic language.* It seems likely that most of the differences

* The well-known language specialist Edward Sapir mentioned once or twice having found evidence of language relationship between Asia and America, but he never published anything on this. Robert Shafer discusses some possible parallels between Athapaskan and Sino-Tibetan in an article entitled "Athapaskan and Sino-Tibetan" in the January, 1952, issue of the *International Journal of American Linguistics,* pages 12-19.

seen in the many languages of the New World came after the people reached America.

Archaeological excavations, even in the damp earth of the Amazon Basin, will in the coming years add to our knowledge of the story of these original Americans. History has passed them by. While other civilizations were growing in Greece and Rome and in the Maya and Inca lands in our own hemisphere, the jungle Indians kept on living in the ancient past. When we come upon them today, it is like finding a keepsake that has survived the ages. The Camayurás are not an ordinary keepsake but a living link with an era so distant that our minds would otherwise have difficulty bridging the gap. To live among them and sense a little of the emotional pattern of their existence, to watch them following a mode of life that may be thousands of years old, necessarily leaves one with a certain feeling of awe, for out of such simple beginnings we have all risen.

We know in general where they came from, and we're finding out how long ago. But how so alert and energetic a people could have failed to reach a higher stage of progress presents an equally intriguing puzzle.

CHAPTER XVIII

RACE OR PLACE

Scientists once thought that people living on a lower stage of development must have lower mental capacities. It was fashionable to describe the native as lacking in powers of concentration and self-restraint. He was a creature of impulse, without forethought or hindsight, dull-witted and insensitive to pain. These conclusions were often voiced by people who had never rubbed elbows with native people, and they have unfortunately been carried over into our own day in popular thought. They have done much to keep us from correctly evaluating the native's powers.

By 1909, the anthropologist Franz Boas had begun to debunk the idea that the mental capacities of primitive people are measurably lower than ours. He and others questioned that the white race had increased its mentality since prehistoric times. We are only separated from the Stone Age by a few hundred generations. Two hundred generations would carry our ancestry back to the invention of the first written language. Our technical and material progress was not to be explained, these anthropologists said, by a sudden increase in brain power. Rather we rose through advantageous techniques that multiply themselves in our spiraling culture.

Where the so-called savage's thought processes appear inferior to ours, we are now inclined to explain it on lack of education. And where his senses seem sharper than ours, as when the native hunter sights an animal before the white man has seen it, we remind ourselves that the native probably knows better where to look and what to look for. In short, there is no positive proof that a native baby, brought up in civilized suroundings exactly as a civilized child, would not show an intellectual development within the normal civilized range.

If the native seems to lack inhibitions, we ask whether it is not simply a difference in his customs. True, most primitive peoples show less restraint about some things than we do; but they also show greater restraint about others. The Camayurá girls might seem to a visitor to be lacking in restraint in regard to sex. But the Camayurás have a strict religious rule against sexual intercourse before a fish-poisoning trip. Native life and thought are so different from ours that comparisons are difficult.

Another great mistake was to call natives childlike. But it was once customary to do so on the grounds that adults low in the cultural scale would resemble the children of people high in it. Adult natives act like adult natives, not like children at all.

Intellectual ability varies greatly among individuals, but racial and tribal averages have not been conclusively shown to differ much.

If we cannot say that a difference in mentality has kept our jungle brothers so simple while we have become so complicated, how are we to explain their backwardness?

We must at this point look at the scientific mistakes of the past. Up to about 1750, scientists trying to explain the many different ways people live on earth were apt to say that God had made the world to meet the needs of every sort of people. Instead of admitting that the Eskimo or the jungle dweller had developed tools and techniques to secure a living under special conditions, they took it for granted that Providence had provided a world that would suit each special taste.

After that, the study of geography found a home in Germany. For the next century, particularly between about 1800 and 1859 when Alexander von Humboldt and Karl Ritter were developing their ideas, the explanations were colored by the philosophical idea of the living unity of nature as propounded by Spinoza and accepted by many other German thinkers. The task was to demonstrate this unity. Humboldt defined it as ". . . a harmony blending together all created things, however dissimilar in form and attributes, one great whole animated by the breath of life." He was angered when someone called him an atheist. He believed rather in a divine spirit that pervaded all things. He said that man is shaped by his surroundings but that not enough evidence had been gathered to lay down rules. He died the year Charles Darwin's *Origin of Species* was published. In that book, for the first time in history, an effort was made to deduce the rules under which plants and animals of all kinds have evolved under the selective influence of their surroundings. Darwin's doctrine of evolution, with incidental adjustments and extensions, is accepted by most biologists today.

Although Darwin attempted to explain the evolution of the animal kingdom, rather than the evolution of man's culture, his doctrine brought the human animal squarely under the microscope. The theological interpretations were thrown into reverse; environment was not providential but demanding. Within ten years, Sir Francis Galton's emphasis on heredity was convincing some people that it was hopeless to try to improve the mind. Social statistics, besides, had begun to reveal an extraordinary regularity in crimes, marriages, and price changes. Everything seemed to show that people were not nearly as free as had been imagined. Natural and economic laws ruled human life. With man's environment blocking him in front and his heredity overtaking him from behind, the mechanistic philosophy of our time was well under way. By 1888, it was not for science but for the poet William Ernest Henley to breast the rising tide with a minority report: "I am the master of my fate; I am the captain of my soul."

Our scientific self-confidence of the twentieth century was yet to develop, and there followed a series of theories offering single causes for human progress. Landscape, climate, race, diet, and health marched across a stage that had previously been lit by the one light of divine guidance. Ellen Semple in her *Influences of Geographic Environment* (1911) said that man is the product of the earth's surface. Its mountainous parts give him strong legs, and the seacoast endows him with a vigorous chest and arms to handle his paddle or oars. Landscape even affects his temperament. Mountain dwellers, according to Ellen Semple, are made conservative by the very nature of their surroundings; subtropical plains dwellers are easygoing, gay, and imaginative.

Ellsworth Huntington stripped away everything he thought unimportant and found climate the determining factor in progress. In his *Civilization and Climate*, first published in 1915, he developed new methods for measuring climatic changes of the past, and he plotted climatic curves beside progress curves. Later, in 1927, while arguing that it was futile to try to separate heredity and environment, he actually gave heredity a boost when he combed *Who's Who* for the secret of our progress and published *The Builders of America*. Others brought heredity into fuzzy focus on a racial basis with their ideas of "Nordic supremacy." (What horrors lay in that direction!) And since it was the superscientific age, it was only natural that some people named science itself as the only thing worth examining as the cause of progress. Life with my jungle brothers gave me time to view these theories in new perspective. Admitting that the influences are many, there might be no harm in asking which one seems the most important. What happened, for instance, 5,000 or 6,000 years ago somewhere in the Middle East that caused a simple farming and herding people to start inventing things that led in rapid order to the great civilizations of Mesopotamia, Egypt, Greece, Rome, the Renaissance, and the industrial civilization of northern Europe and America? The change came only an instant ago in the geologic time scale, and the earth was a long time waiting for it.

The age of the earth is now thought to be 3½ billion years. It was announced in *Science*, April 16, 1954, that life of some sort must have existed on earth 2½ billion years ago, as revealed by biogenic carbon isotopes. It surprises some people to know that man has missed so much of the show. The human race has been on earth only one five-thousandth as long as other forms of life. And man spent something like 99/100ths of this time in reaching the point where he could build the pyramids of Egypt. Another way of saying this is that if we mark off on the face of a clock all the time that has passed since life began on earth, man's entire period would be only about nine seconds. The Egyptians would have built their pyramids only one-tenth of a second ago. On our geologic clock, the things that dominate our lives—the airplane, the automobile, radio, motion pictures, television, and atomic science—would all have been invented in one-thousandth of a second. When we ask what started all this a fraction of a second ago, as it were, we are not asking a trivial question.

The Camayurás wondered why I sat facing the dying colors of the sunset out over Lake Ipavú while the life of the evening was starting around their central campfire. Against the immensity of space with its infinite worlds, I felt even less willing than before to suppose that those of us who chance to live at this pinpoint in time and space have quite as full a monopoly on important things as we are apt to believe. It would be too much of a coincidence for us to have hit the cosmic jackpot, satisfying though the thought might be.

Tah-koo-mah, who had been fixing the bone point to an arrow, had laid aside his work to join the campfire revelries. Clearly he didn't believe that anything else in the world was important. What one thing that these people lacked would have made the greatest difference to them if they had had it? It was easy to think of various objects that would have made a difference—the wheel, an ox to plow the field, a blade or point of metal. But since man's greatest advances are mental rather than physical, I decided that it would be a mental tool rather than a physical one. Perhaps the thing that would be most important to technical progress as we know it would be writing.

Even the simplest beginnings of writing must have been important to people who previously had had to remember everything. Imagine trying to keep our civilization alive with only such knowledge as can be passed down from father to son by word of mouth, without the books on medicine, engineering, and electronics, without the records of commercial dealings and the legal papers that put promises on record, without everything from the grocery list to the million parts that go into a modern air liner. Primitive people have to remember how to make all their tools, how to hunt different kinds of animals and to fish, how to plant and take care of crops if there is gardening, how to convert natural materials into clothing (in this tribe nil), and a great deal more about the products of the forest or field. Besides this knowledge, they transmit from father to son a large mass of superstition and ceremonial lore.

True, in the New Stone Age there was specialization of work, which gave some people one kind of knowledge to keep and others another. But even with this help, there was a limit without writing.

Art can develop without writing. Even the "literary arts" can. Some of the Polynesian chants, for example, possess high aesthetic quality, and many tribes have been admired for the spiritual and philosophical sensitivity of their formal speeches. But the seeds of the technical civilization that surrounds and influences us every moment of our lives were sown when written language was born.

The invention of writing enabled people to give their time to reasoning rather than to remembering. Writing made it possible to carry on business. Unfinished trading operations could be recorded; account could be kept of what one man owed another. Writing laid the foundation for a new economic system, and we have been following it with variations ever since. Written records are the backbone of the ownership of land and other property, of commerce, the lending of goods and money, banking, and more recently of a new form of property, the ownership of ideas as protected through patents. A primitive medicine man sometimes owns a magic word, a phrase, or an idea as part of his art. But a whole tribe can only have a few pieces of abstract property of this sort, limited by human memory. Each word or song that the medicine man uses does not have back of it a numbered document as do the 2,000,000 patents in the United States Patent Office.

Of all of these things, my jungle brothers knew absolutely nothing. Without arithmetic, (the language of numbers), written laws, court records, medical formulas, a calendar to go by—without any knowledge of the world beyond what they had seen or been told about—they could not progress technically much beyond where our ancestors stood something like 10,000 years ago.

Various peoples in different localities have invented writing, so we cannot say that this master key to progress depends upon either race or place. The first real writing seems to have been invented in southern Mesopotamia almost exactly 5,000 years ago. The Egyptians began to write about the same time, the Chinese not until about 1,500 years later. The Mayas seem not to have evolved their written language as far as they did their science of numbers. The Aztecs created one of the few complex cultures of early times without a written language.

Perhaps the hardest thing to get our hand on in a study like this is the inner spirit that causes people to *want* to change or improve themselves. If we explain away all the negative hindrances to human advancement, we come upon the very essence of man himself—the thing that makes him different from all other creatures. It is the will to win against natural obstacles and to prepare for new events in wide variety. Many things can prevent man from succeeding, but given a reasonably productive homeland and average or better than average mental and physical endowment, there yet remains one thing—an abstract thing in his nature—without which he will not better himself. If life is either satisfactory or hopeless, people will show no spirit to change. There may have been a little of both elements in the outlook of the Camayurás.

A population ordinarily increases until it reaches the limits of the existing food supply. Here there were illimitable forests that could be cleared for farming, yet the people seemed to be under no pressure to enlarge their gardens. I was puzzled by the scarcity of Indians over fifty years of age. There were a lot of children and a great many young couples in their twenties or early thirties, but there were few in this village even above forty. Perhaps intertribal warfare took a greater toll than I realized. Perhaps, in spite of their vigor, their age limit was kept down by some illness or parasitic affliction I could not detect. Perhaps the lack of old people was only a temporary unbalance due to some epidemic. I cannot yet say. But there must be something that is holding their population in check and thus removing one of the pressures that cause people to try to better their lot.

CHAPTER XIX

MY COMPASS AND MY KNIFE

All the stars were now out, and I showed Tah-koo-mah my compass. Colonel Fawcett had made a mistake in deceiving the Kalapalos about his compass. He told them that it showed him at any time from which direction he might expect his enemies. The Indians at once wanted so valuable an instrument, and their desire to own it, together with certain other grievances, led to his murder. I was determined to avoid that mistake, but I got into an embarrassing situation just the same.

The Southern Cross stood out brightly in the clear sky, and I showed Tah-koo-mah that the needle always pointed to it. He told me that they had never seen or heard of such an instrument. A number of other men of the village crowded around me. Their low talking voiced great curiosity.

"Perhaps you do not believe," I said, "that it will still point to those stars if we go to the other side of the clearing."

They dragged me to the other side. But I had been sitting on a tiny folding camp stool that I had, and they wouldn't let me show the compass again until my stool had been brought. They talked excitedly when they saw the needle find the Southern Cross. We moved to various places around the village. Each time the stool had to be put under me before they would let me show the compass.

I then said, "Now I will give the explanation."

This was more than they had bargained for. It was also

more than I had planned for. Tah-koo-mah's brother, who was trying to learn Portuguese, echoed the wishes of the rest by explosively repeating, "*Explicaçao! Explicaçao!*"

But I had come to class without my lesson. "The force that pulls the needle is not in the stars but in the earth," I began.

"In the earth," repeated Tah-koo-mah, exerting every brain cell.

"It is also in the needle," I went on.

"What force?" asked Tah-koo-mah.

"The force is something like electricity," I said. I was only getting in deeper.

It would have been easy to tell them that the compass had a spirit in it, and they would have understood perfectly. But I let this round go to the Camayurás. The men were disappointed, and they drifted off into the shadows. I took Tah-koo-mah aside and asked him to give the compass privately to his father. I never showed seven others I had brought along for trading.

When traveling light, it is hard to arm oneself against the boredom of a lonely journey. There isn't room for reading matter. Unlike Diogenes, I was not even carrying a lantern. But I had formed a plan that worked well. It was based on the simple fact that recording tapes weigh no more with radio programs on them than they do empty, and they are easily cleared for reuse. So during the two weeks before leaving home, I recorded some favorite programs onto my tapes, without listening to them.

That night, wearied by the wonders about me, I lay for perhaps two hours with the headphones, enjoying murder mysteries, comedians, and classical music as the mood moved me. I listened to the voices of Groucho Marx, Ezio Pinza, Edgar Bergen, and Bob Hope, while around the campfire I heard wild chants that seemed to come from the dawn of human history. Listening to the tapes turned out to be more of an emotional experience than I had bargained for, because in recording the programs the recorder had picked up things it wasn't supposed to. In the middle of "Gang Busters," the voice of our little daughter Rodi broke through as she burst into the room with a playmate. Then in the middle of a quiz program, I could hear Susie practicing "Caro Mio Ben" at the piano in the living room. Perhaps Susie and Rodi were at this minute taking Blackie out for her nightly airing on 77th Street and looking up at the same moon that was shining so brightly into this jungle clearing.

When I laid the earphones down, I saw that my jungle brothers were looking at me from the edges of their hammocks. The machine still fascinated them, and their faces showed they thought that the man who used it was a strange one. They jabbered and laughed, and seeing that I liked it here were willing to let it go at that.

How could I have explained to them what it was like at the corner of Broadway and 42nd Street? They knew nothing of how our nerves are bombarded by advertisers, moralists, entertainers, gag writers. Buttons to bring pills or postage stamps, buttons to open doors, doors that open without buttons. Buttons to produce theatre tickets, sandwiches, cola drinks; buttons to tell how much weight we've gained and whether we're lucky in love. Buttons that will print our names on a metal disk; buttons in automatic restaurants, buttons that count when you push them; buttons that turn H. V. Kaltenborn into Milton Berle on a glass screen. Buttons that bring the elevator, and buttons that have stopped working and won't bring anything.

My friends in the other hammocks would be surprised if they could shoot through the earth in a subway. The last of the commuters, I realized, would be reaching their homes about now. The advertising cards in the cars would have done their duty for the day, telling them how to hold their bodies in shape; how to get rid of their headaches; how to cure their indigestion.

My companions in the hut, having eaten heavily, were now getting rid of their intestinal gas, and there was nothing in Camayurá etiquette that required even Koo-yah-yoo, the most beautiful girl in the tribe, to be quiet about it. She was leaning out of her hammock and blowing the embers of the fire between us. When I suggested by sign language that she could keep two fires going, one in front and one behind, she got the point quickly, smiled, and seemed modestly pleased that I should notice her capacities.

I have doubted that city life allows the human spirit to grow. My brother, who is a city man, disagrees. "If you lived in the Golden Age of Pericles," he asks, "would you live somewhere away out in the sticks, or in Athens where everything was happening? New York is the place today." He has a point, but I was having so much fun in the wilderness that I was looking doubtfully at the price tag on the average nine-to-five job. You couldn't live among simple, natural people like these Camayurás without looking with fresh doubt on some of the things we call "modern living."

I believed it was to my advantage not to fool these Indians or set myself up as a wizard. However, I did have a trick penknife, which couldn't be opened if you didn't know how, and I couldn't resist showing it to them the next day. The knife took their interest immediately. I jokingly told them that their fingers were not strong enough to pull the blade out and that they ought to take more exercise. I could open the blade easily in one movement, but every time I gave the knife back to one of these muscular men of nature, he would strain away at it and break his fingernails trying to pull the blade out.

Everybody had to have a chance, and this went on and on. All that was necessary to open the knife was to turn it upside down and push the blade in instead of pulling it out. The men all got to laughing and grabbing it out of each other's hands, each certain that he could win the praise of all by getting the blade out. They couldn't really have thought that my fingers were stronger, but they kept on trying to open the knife by brute force.

An Eskimo, earlier experience told me, would have found the secret of how to open the knife by now. The Camayurás were alert and eager, but even after I had shown them how to do it, they didn't understand. I had to go through the motion slowly several times before they caught on. All who know the Eskimos remark on how ingenious they are, and the ones I had been with some years before were much quicker about mechanical things than these Camayurás. In an Eskimo village in Alaska where I once spent a month or two, intelligence tests had shown that there were more children of exceptional ability among them than in the average group of American children. My friend Richard Harrington tried the Eskimos out with wire puzzles and was likewise impressed with how fast they solved them.

The mental alertness and ingenuity of the Eskimo is often explained on a basis of his hard Arctic environment. Actually, the Eskimos, equipped as they are with clothing and dwellings that protect them from the winter cold, live under less difficult conditions than people often imagine. But perhaps only those who were mentally equal to the challenge moved into the northern regions and stayed there. And in developing the tools, clothing, and dwellings that they now have, it is possible that those who were slow and stupid perished along the way. This selective process may have caused a gradual rise in the average intelligence. But I believe there is a stronger reason.

When an Eskimo baby is born, it is given the name of a highly thought-of relative who has recently died—a wise old aunt or an uncle or grandfather who was a great hunter or medicine man. When the baby gets this name he gets the spirit or soul of the person who had it last. Most important, the child also gets the respect that the grown-ups had for the original owner of the name. A little baby a few months old may even be called "uncle" or "grandfather." This leads to a parent-child relationship different from any I have seen or heard of elsewhere. The Eskimo father or mother will never strike a child or scold it roughly. This is because they are afraid of causing the name-soul to leave the child, which would cause it to sicken and die. Eskimo children are among the most pampered—and least hampered—children in the world. The father and mother would not think of questioning the judgment of the wise old soul. Even when a two-year-old baby begins to poke the blade of a sharp knife into its mouth, the parents do not stop it.

The Eskimos grow up knowing that a knife can hurt them but that their parents won't. They have been allowed to try everything out for themselves and learn by experience. Theirs is the psychology of try-try instead of don't-don't. I think that this builds up in them the self-reliance, friendliness, and resourcefulness that so many travelers have spoken of.

The northern Indians who live closest to the Eskimos spend the early part of their lives tied to a cradle board, unable to reach anything and examine it. The Eskimo child is the most important person in a social gathering, but the Indian baby is stood up in the corner out of the way. For long periods, the Indian baby lives a life that we would enforce only upon someone who was violently insane. Of course, under normal circumstances, children learn to walk and talk and do other things according to a certain timetable. But it seems quite likely that certain things in their upbringing like those just mentioned influence their personalities. These strait-jacketed papooses seem to grow up into exactly what one would expect—sullen, uncooperative adults, blocked by inward hostilities and poorly equipped to work their way out of an emergency. The Eskimo, on the other hand, if he has been brought up in the age-old pattern of beliefs, meets life's problems with swift wisdom and a generosity of spirit that reaches out even to the stranger on the trail.

Perhaps there is a lesson in this for us. Perhaps it extends beyond the parent-child relationship to our attitudes about more distant people who happen to be different in "age" or stage of progress. I am not recommending one half of the Eskimo child-care policy (the no-punishment part) without the other half (love for the child and respect for its soul). There is nothing in the Eskimo's attitude that says, "The brat will damned well find out for himself." Rather, the effect is like the broadest willingness to call the baby an individual in his own right, heir to abilities and virtues which, though not fully apparent in so weak a body, make him from the start an entity and a personality. In the deep love that exists between Eskimo parents and children I never saw signs of the emotional bondage that keeps many persons in our world from growing happily out of childhood and into marriage and parenthood. I doubt that we would see so many adults who have never outgrown childish emotions if parents loved their children enough to be willing to let them grow up.

The Camayurás make a lot of their children. They treat them with more understanding than many a mother seen in a New York park and with not so much measured solicitude as those who stroke the child with one hand while holding in the other a book that tells them how important it is to love. But they do not treat their children as Eskimos do. On two occasions while I was living with the Camayurás, I saw a mother (never a father) shake or cuff a youngster. The younger Camayurás seemed to be under more discipline in the broad sense than the Eskimo youths. Perhaps this is partly because the Eskimos have no chiefs in the sense that these jungle Indians do. Even though the Camayurá chief is not the strong-arm type, he is clearly the symbol of authority in the village and gives it a unity which in the Eskimo community may not go beyond the family.

CHAPTER XX

ECONOMIC REVOLUTION AT IPAVÚ

The ideas of the Camayurás seemed to differ from ours mostly on sex and property. Lack of opportunity to gain position or power through wealth gives them a different outlook. With us, a thousand pressures urge us to buy the car or house or television set that will make our neighbor envious. Perhaps these pressures give our judgment and sense of right or wrong a better chance to develop. But with the Camayurás, they are almost absent. Each family has its canoe, thatched hut, and tools. No one has gained a sewing machine or an outboard motor for the others to envy. Bows must be traded for pottery, or hammocks for flutes. There is no money, so there is no need to show how much one can buy.

The nearest thing to money was the string of shells some of them wore around the waist. The shells were from fresh-water mussels, shaped into thin disks about three-eighths of an inch in diameter, with a hole in the center. Blue trade beads are taking their place. There wern't many of either. And to our way of thinking, there wasn't much in the village to buy with them.

Everybody seemed to have the necessities; there were few luxuries. The most powerful man was the chief, but his things seemed to be more everybody's than anyone else's were. The Camayurás have great capacity for acquisitiveness; but as I saw them, they didn't need much or have much, and there wasn't any apparent desire for one man to claim that he was worth more than another economically. Respect and authority were gained through age and wisdom in matters affecting the good of the group, and the chieftainship was dependent at least partly on birth. Women took a lesser part in group affairs but did not seem to be ill treated.

This change from money to barter is one of the most noticeable things when you enter the life of people like these. I had been urged in Rio to leave my money in safekeeping, but because I might be flown out to a different city on my return where I would be helpless without cash, I had carried it. Here it was worthless.

I had delayed trading as long as possible in the hope of keeping my bargaining power. When I couldn't stall any longer, I told the Indians we would do business the next day. When the time came, I marked a line on the ground and showed them I meant to trade across it. But it wasn't long before they let me know that they wanted another method. Could it be that I was expected to show all my things first? I had never run into this sort of thing with natives.

I opened with gifts for the children. First came the yo-yos and bubble-blowing sets. Soon the air of the clearing was dancing with iridescent bubbles, and the tribesmen, their wives, and children were full of joy. This was when I came closest to becoming a medicine man. The bubbles were still floating around above the thatched huts when the balloons started to pop. I had brought a hundred of them. Each time there was an explosion, a shout would go up. Although they couldn't understand what I was saying, I kept up a running chatter. The cheers got louder, and every time another balloon went off I would call out, "Another Indian bit the dust!" Then everybody would laugh. I didn't mind hearing the balloons go. But a wildness was coming over the group. I was only trying to put over a business deal, but it began to look as though it might be easier to lead an attack against the Suyás.

The Indians kept asking for more and giving nothing. I hadn't expected anything in exchange for the toys, but I certainly did when it came to the mirrors, watertight match cases, ribbons, plastic bags, nylon cord, soap, fishhooks, and many other things. It began to look as though they were shaking me down.

There was a cartoon in *The New Yorker* that showed one explorer saying to his companion, with the trade goods spread out in front of them, "Does it occur to you that they might be bright enough to realize they can get all this stuff for nothing?" I was in that fix, but I didn't have anyone to talk to about it. The Indians were getting more and more excited. Still, everything was under control—until I brought out my needles.

No one had told me I should bring needles. Among people who had no cloth of any kind and did no sewing or weaving, one wouldn't expect that needles would be valuable. But they were. The Indians had always had to use a fish tooth for sewing the feathers on their arrows. When I brought out steel needles, they forgot everything else. And I had brought only two packages—rather for my own use than to bring about an industrial revolution on the upper Xingu.

The few needles vanished in an instant. A moment later, I wouldn't have recognized the proud monopolists who got all of them or the frenzied poor who had none as the same people who shortly before had been splashing each other gaily in the lake without a care in the world. There had always been plenty of fish teeth, but here was something better in small supply.

"More needles," said Tah-koo-mah.

At first I thought I could keep them from knowing that I had no more. I waved the question aside. The other things I had shown were either so far beyond their accustomed ways that the Indians didn't react to them or I had enough to go around. Not so with the needles. They produced the first sign of envy I had seen and the beginnings of the peace of mind that comes from having economic advantage. I had sown the seeds of class warfare and was getting a glimpse of what it would be like when the white man's gadget civilization broke through in full force to these people.

"They want more needles," repeated Tah-koo-mah.

I then told him there weren't any. The news made him distinctly unhappy. Since the monopolists were becoming more and more unpopular, I decided on a sharp change of strategy, hoping to bring the people back into a recreational mood and draw them together again into the common bonds of brotherhood. This meant parting with my prize object, the thing I had meant to keep to the end. I had picked it up in New York one day while strolling the streets, pondering what kind of things a jungle Indian would like. I knew they all swam, not only for fun but in pursuit of arrowed fish. Would not a diving mask please them? It was clear at the bottom of my bag, but I dug it out.

I did not know at this time that the Camayurás had murdered Albert de Winton and that his bones lay at the bottom of the lake. When I showed them the diving mask and explained how it let you see everything underwater, they only looked at each other and didn't seem interested. The diving mask was spirited away, and I never saw it again.

They thawed out again when I brought out my clown paints and demonstrated them on one of the women. The Camayurás had only red and black body paint, so this theatrical kit was the same as giving them a whole drygoods store. I half expected them to use up all the coloring at once in an orgy of trying on this and that, but they only sampled the wonderful stuff sparingly and put it away.

Anyway, all were cheerful when I handed out my last mirror and closed the zipper on my bag. I kept only a few strings of beads and the like for bartering my way through the country in case the need arose. I then lay down in my hammock, wondering whether their courtesy covered up a form of theft.

But after awhile, they began to bring things in. Flutes, bows and arrows, animal-shaped bowls, equipment for processing manioc, and so on. Why had they not been willing to exchange item for item? Natives usually like to make a game of it, and they can be very shrewd. They will hold back their best things until your trade goods have run out and then get you to part with your shirt and hunting knife. These people had not cheated me. They had willingly brought me a wide assortment of their best things and seemed anxious that I should be pleased. I decided that, since practically everything I had was new to them, they had been embarrassed about suggesting equivalents. They were certainly the most innocent of people. I tied a tag on each object as they gave it to me so that the things would not get mixed up with the household objects around the hut.

At intervals all that afternoon they brought me stuff. The next day, when it slowed down, I said, "Tah-koo-mah, there is one more thing I want—most of all. One of your beautiful red and yellow feather headdresses."

"Impossible!" he said flatly.

I thought I must have touched upon something sacred. But the headdress was the most spectacular thing they had, and an hour or so later I said again how disappointed I was not to have one. His answer shows how much these people live in the moment and how strongly their interest is centered on the matter at hand.

"We can't possibly give it to you," he said, "because we are going to use it today. Come around afterward."

After the dance, I didn't have to ask them for the headdress. They brought it to me and didn't even expect anything in exchange.

Tah-koo-mah and I sometimes tried to teach his sister some Portuguese, but we didn't get far. I often took a swim late in the afternoon at the foot of the path, 100 yards from the village. Perhaps so she could borrow my soap, Koo-yah-yoo would appear from nowhere, shy but sure of herself. (In place of soap, she only had a wad of coarse grasslike stuff.) I would wash her back and she would wash mine. Nothing her parents or fellow villagers may have told her made her afraid of me. One afternoon, a man who seemed more worldly-wise than the others appeared to be joking with her over how dangerous I was. She gave him a look that said as plainly as words, "You take care of your dangers, and I'll take care of mine."

I never saw the young people in the village making love, and I couldn't tell whether Koo-yah-yoo had a boy friend. If so, she didn't hesitate to decorate herself when I was the only one around. Once, while she was lying with one leg over the edge of her hammock, she took an *urucú* pod, the source of their red body paint, and rolled it gently back and forth between her fingers until the insides were juicy and the pointed end cracked open. Then she stuck a delicately frayed straw into it, moistened the end with the oily coloring matter, and proceeded to draw a design on her thigh. She used only the smallest amount of paint and touched the tip of the straw so gently to her skin that I asked her whether it didn't tickle, scratching my own leg to show what I meant. She only smiled and twirled the feathered end of her tiny brush again in the oozing pod, and went on with her painting. Finally, I said, "See here, if you spend the evening painting, you'll be late to the dance. You'll find me outside where it's a little cooler." I think she had great understanding. She never seemed to miss my meaning, though she had only the tone of my voice and my gestures to go by.

Weeks later, in a Rio penthouse, some friends wanted me to tell them about these Indians, and I described Koo-yah-yoo. The wife of a United States general remarked how sad it was to think what she might have been if she could have enjoyed a few of the advantages of civilization. I'm not so sure.

She is happy and healthy on the shores of Lake Ipavú. She is in tune with nature and with the society of her fellow man. We imagine that our civilization can do so much to help the people of the wild. Our medical knowledge can; perhaps also some of our ethical philosophy—if we follow it well enough to teach it. But the before-and-after pictures show that we have not learned through the centuries how to meet native races without hurting them. We insist on putting clothes on them, which a day later are dirty and unsanitary. Diseases that are not usually serious with us kill or cripple them in great numbers. They lose their own culture and the pleasure of their traditions, and we give them little beyond the chance to become second-class citizens.

Civilized people, I suppose, are people who wear clothes. On that basis, one might call these people savages, because the complete outfit of the well-dressed debutante on Lake Ipavú weighed one-twentieth of an ounce. Yet they showed nothing in their entertainment patterns like our emphasis on sex. I saw no pornography, no "burlesque."

The psychology and sex life of these people has been adjusted for countless centuries to a complete absence of clothing. I'm not sure that Koo-yah-yoo, if she could watch us, would think us exactly proper. The least we can do is to keep from calling naked people like these immodest. They were charmingly modest about their workmanship and cooking. What they lacked was shame.

I had begun by distrusting these people and ended by being flattered beyond words when the chief and others asked me four times whether I was going to come back.

The last time I saw Koo-yah-yoo, I passed her on the trail outside the village. I had gone for a stroll at sun-up before leaving. She was going out and I was coming in. A glance passed between us, and she gave me her fleeting smile. She was saying good-by to the strange white man. I was saying good-by to the world of yesterday.

Koo-yah-yoo may never see a Cadillac or a Bendix, but one has to have more faith in civilization than I do to wish her all our so-called advantages, including a husband who might leave her for a global war. She'll be happier with a man who can shoot fish with an arrow and build a home out of what's at hand than with one who would exhaust himself seeking a kind of security she wouldn't understand and striving to gain freedoms she never lost.

CHAPTER XXI

A THIEF AND A FREE MAN

I had worried about getting back to Jacaré, thinking of the two places where a boat was needed and wondering whether my jungle brothers, after getting most of my trade goods, would care whether I made it or not. But they were good friends and saw me back, not as many of them nor as gay a party.

Along the dusty trail across the upland, I had only one bad experience. Somehow the Indians must have gone off the trail near the start, possibly to gather *urucú*, because I got ahead of them without knowing it and for some miles wore myself out trying to catch up when they were really behind me all the time. The heat was sweltering, and soon I had drunk all the water in my canteen. In time, I grew really anxious. Perhaps they had forked off on a different route. I was still on the right track, because there were the boot prints I had left on the way in.

When I got to the swamp where my footprints ended, I knew it was the same spot where we had been on the journey in, but no Indians were anywhere to be seen. If by any chance the Indians were all ahead of me, they would get to the other end of the swamp where the canoe was and find me missing. I could only hope that they would then come back. I sat down to rest and wait.

It must have been almost half an hour before I heard voices from behind and, looking up, saw my friends coming. When

I told them that I had thought they were all ahead, they couldn't explain it. So through the swamp we waded, laughing over the mistake, and we took it easy paddling the hidden river at the other end, trying to shoot fish close to the shore.

All the while I was wondering whether I could now camp on Orlando Villas Boas' trail long enough to catch him on his way back to the Tuatuarí. I hoped that he had not already returned to his village, because with almost all of my trade goods gone it would not be easy to get a canoe and some Indians to take me there.

Upon arriving at Jacaré, I was relieved to learn from some of the Indians there that he had not been seen and must still be down the Xingu. So I settled in an empty hut and prepared to wait. I was now already overdue from the office, but having spent six months on the idea of meeting him, I couldn't let him slip through my hands now if another week or so would turn the trick.

The Indian village at Jacaré was interesting, but it included members of several tribes from round about, and there were already signs of decay in the native personality, even though this spot was only in slight touch with civilization by air. Back at Ipavú I had often marveled at the inherent honesty with which the Camayurás had treated me. I wished there were some way whereby they could avoid the temptations that our civilization almost always brings. Primitive people quickly learn to beg and then to steal. The beginnings of this process could be seen at Jacaré. Once when I was in my hammock I saw the form of a man, silent as a ghost, bending to look through some cracks in the wall of my hut. There was only one door to this hut, and I had put all my equipment and what was left of my trade goods against the back wall. To lessen the possibility of theft, I had strung my two hammocks across the hut in such a position that anyone going to where the duffel bags were would have to crawl under both of them. When the Indians knew I was in the hut, they often came in and sat on the dirt floor and stared. They always left when I did, and I had never found one inside upon returning.

On this occasion, I had almost fallen asleep when I noticed the stealthy figure outside. Thinking at first that I was about to have a friendly visitor, I paid no attention. But he didn't see me, or else he thought I was asleep, for instead of going to the door, as would be normal, he went around to the back of the hut, right outside the place where my goods were stored. Soon I heard him working at the wall, and in no time he was removing a whole section.

This was the first time an Indian had tried to take anything from me. I spoke in English, as fast as possible. "What do you think you are doing?" I said. "If you think you can take this house apart, you're mistaken. You can start right in putting it back together again."

The Indian was as surprised as I was. He set right to work putting the wall back in place. He didn't take long to get it in order again and quietly disappeared. I often saw him afterward in the village, and we would greet each other with knowing glances.

"Some of them will steal," admitted Senhor Alencar at the lonely air strip at Jacaré. One day his wife Dona Lucia, a warmhearted and hospitable woman with two babies, confided that she didn't like the Indians.

"What a place to live," I said, "if you don't like Indians."

But she seemed otherwise to enjoy life here, though there wasn't another white woman within 200 miles. Her home was a large grass-covered hut. On one side of the central living and eating room was the kitchen and storeroom, on the other the bedroom and radio space. We ate at a circular table covered with a tasseled plush coverlet, relics of the old life brought into the jungle. Indian dance masks, bows and arrows, and rattles hung from the roof. Water had to be carried from a large rope-and-bucket well that Alencar had dug, and the drinking water dripped through a terra cotta filter of a type common in Brazil. Dona Lucia's larder was limited to small game that Alencar brought in from the forest or fish shot by the Indians, but they grew their own vegetables and corn. She cooked wonderful meals on a raised earth hearth, often breast-feeding her infant and keeping up a running conversation at the same time. She was the first white woman to have given birth to a child so far in the interior. The little girl had been born in Chavantina, the year-old boy here.

When I gave her some of my dehydrated foods, she made them taste like something the chef at the Ritz might have turned out. One might have thought that another mouth to feed would have been a burden, but my presence seemed to be the excuse for delicacies beyond what would ordinarily have been thought necessary.

It takes good humor and inner strength to live the life Dona Lucia had chosen. She was the kind by whom the foundations of our country were built. No beauty parlors or cocktail parties for her. Plenty of work, the solace of nature, her growing babies, and the love of a good man were her life. I never saw her go farther than the well. She had made a reasonably comfortable and seemingly happy life with the simple resources the wilderness offered, and she never complained. Among their few luxuries brought in by airplane was a brand-new short wave radio. It would bring in broadcasts from Rio and Buenos Aires about 1,000 miles away.

We held long midnight conversations in a philosophical mood, by the flickering light from a bottle of kerosene with a ropelike wick sticking out of the top. And always there were the Indians, moving in the shadows.

Senhor Alencar was a wiry woodsman, and he went hunting every afternoon at five. Sometimes I went along, not to hunt but to learn more about Mato Grosso. When I told him that people in the United States had asked me to find out what it would be like to homestead here, he gave a spirited speech in favor of the idea: "Plenty of fine rich soil, abundant game, innumerable rivers of pure clear water, a fine climate . . ." and so on. "Nor is there any place in the world," he went on, "where you can get farther from the threat of the atom bomb or from the enemy." (I hadn't known until now whom he meant by "the enemy," but it was plain he meant communism.) "I shall be the last to defend the freedom of man." he said, patting his rifle. "If, in spite of all we pray for, communism spreads around the world, it will find me ready to fight it. I shall be the last free man on earth. I shall go down in history as the last anti-Communist. They'll have to put up a monument to me."

I dared to suggest that they might instead put up a monument to the Communist who killed him.

"No," he said, "too many will fall before they take me. In common decency, they will honor only one hero."

Through a week of waiting here at Jacaré, I kept remembering Colonel Eggeling's words: "Time is your enemy." June 9 was approaching, and many things—failure of Orlando's outboard motor, illness, or accident—could delay him beyond that day when the last plane I could possibly wait for would go.

While I lay in my hammock in that hut at Jacaré, I tried to picture the man of mystery I had come to see. From the bits of his career that I had pieced together, I knew that he had been born in the town of Botucatu in the state of São Paulo, the son of a back-country lawyer. He was working for one of the oil companies in 1943 when he applied for a position on the famous Roncador-Xingu Expedition, and that was when his fabulous career began. The purpose of the expedition was to make emergency air strips on the Great Diagonal from Rio de Janeiro across the Amazon Basin to Caracas, Venezuela, and Miami, cutting across the bulge of Brazil and saving many hours and much gasoline. The most frightening obstacle that lay in the path of this short cut was the territory of the Chavante Indians.

This was before any of these most dangerous of all Brazilian Indians had been brought into peaceful relations. Two years before, Genésio Pimentel Barbosa and his five companions, while trying to give peace offerings to the Chavantes, had been clubbed to death and cut to pieces by them in this territory. In the same year, Orlando Villas Boas' mother and father both died, and he put in his application for a place on the expedition, though he must have known that it was the most expertly trained group ever to explore the Amazon. It was to have some sixty scientists, technicians, scouts, and frontiersmen, all under the leadership of Colonel Flaviano Mattos Vanique. The purposes of this expedition were similar to those of our Lewis and Clark Expedition, but its scientific tools overshadowed the grandest dreams of those who opened our own West.

To Orlando Villas Boas, the undiscovered lands beyond the frontier were only a name. But someone must have known a born explorer when he saw one, for Orlando was chosen from the many applicants. So were his younger brothers Leonardo and Cláudio. Measured by the results, Fate must be said at this point to have thrust a hand into the stormy history of the largest remaining wilderness in the Western Hemisphere.

From the start of the expedition, Orlando Villas Boas distinguished himself through his ability to get along in the jungle and to deal with dangerous Indians. It was not long before he volunteered to lead an advance guard of sixteen men, a spearhead to cut a trail through the stronghold of the Chavante Indians. This was the land between the Rio das Mortes and the Xingu, an area as large as New Hampshire and Vermont, and hideous in reputation.

It took Orlando and his companions six months to make the journey, but when he reappeared at Chavantina, his men had cleared the ground for two air strips in the middle of the wilderness and had reached the Rio Sete de Setembro, a tributary of the Xingu—all this without losing a man. From that time on, Orlando's jungle know-how and his remarkable talent with the natives kept him at the very front of the advance to the northwest. In the wilderness far to the north of Jacaré, the expedition, with strong support from the Brazilian Air Force, made an air strip in the Serra do Cachimbo, which anchored the axis of the Great Diagonal. It had taken four years. When the expedition finished its work and returned to civilization six years ago, Orlando Villas Boas chose to stay in the jungle.

I was trying to weigh the qualities of a man who could endure so many years of hardship and danger, and trying to picture his physical appearance, when, about 11 o'clock in the morning, in he walked—without any shoes or shirt.

finished Camayurá hut and one under construction. The thick thatching sheds opical downpours but permits ventilation. The huts form a circle or oval around ne central clearing and have one door in front and another behind, opening to ne forest. Inside the hut, the hammocks are strung from the two central poles to l parts of the wall, like the spokes of a wheel. The man below is sorting palm bres that his wife will use in completing the half-finished hammock directly behind him.

The chief's daughter, Koo-yah-yoo in her hammock in the central hut.

The author recording native music with his portable tape recorder. Weighing only about fifteen pounds with its own batteries, it served also as a robot secretary.

Two Camayurá women processing manioc, the poisonous relative of our tapioca plant. The one at left is scraping the tuberous roots, which are bundled in the foreground; the woman at right is grating them on a board set with nail-like thorns from the trunk of a palm tree.

Iere Koo-yah-yoo is squeezng the grated pulp of manioc to remove the poison.

The pulp is squeezed in a matting over a pottery bowl almost a yard in diameter.

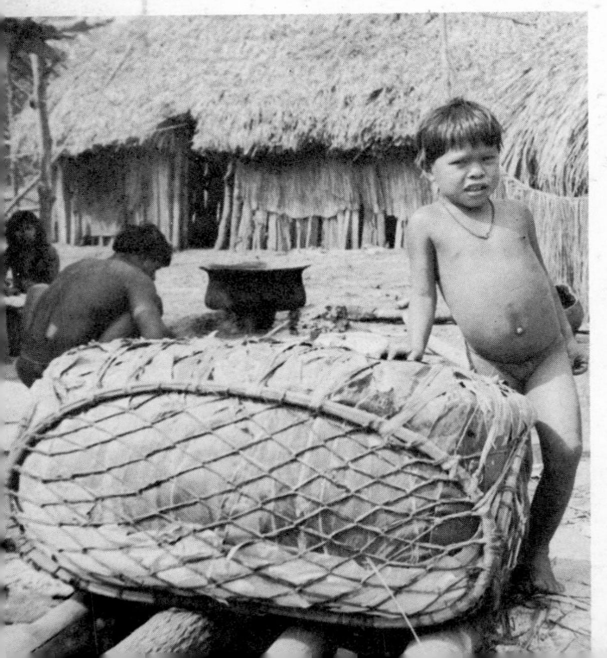

When processed, the ma
is molded into bricks (
the feet of the child at l
or stored in leaf-lined bas
like the one shown here
use in future months

Sunset over Lake Ipavú, while the village prepared for the revelries of the night.

Orlando Villas Boas, friend of the Indians, who has made himself at home in one of the wildest parts of the earth.

Orlando wading ashore at Jacaré after a long trip by dugout down the Xingu River. In the stern of the boat is his brother Cláudio.

rlando Villas Boas feeding pet eagle kept in a conical ge typical among the Xingu ibes.

A friendly Indian of Xingu demonstrating a club and headdress of hostile Tumurí tribe

Three Xingu Indians at Jacaré making music at night for the author's tape recorder.

CHAPTER XXII

BAREFOOTED AMBASSADOR

He was a pint-sized Robinson Crusoe with a jet black beard and the eyes of a mystic. His only clothing was a pair of ragged pants. His body was deeply sun-tanned, and on his head sat a bleached and shrunken canvas hat. He looked about 35 years old, and he weighed only 115 pounds.

This was the man who was virtual ruler of an area the size of New England.

"I offer you my respects," I said in Portuguese. "Have you traveled far?"

"Nearly 300 miles down the Xingu and back. Word got through to me that you were coming, and I waited eight days, hoping you could go with us, but the rivers were falling and we had to leave. Will you come to our village?"

Soon we were in his dugout, heading up the Kuluene River toward the kind of a camp that the Indian Service calls a "point of approach," that is, an outpost in the wilderness from which an attempt will be made to get in touch with unknown tribes.

During the days I was with Orlando, I began to understand what Lewis Cotlow, the author of *Amazon Headhunters*, had told me. He had crossed trails with Orlando once and had entered an Indian village with him. "Just because I was with Orlando," he said, "the Indians were at once friendly with me. . . . There is something in his presence. I can only call it love."

I was beginning to realize how much my own friendly reception among the Indians of this region may have been due to the trust created by this one man. Centuries of cruelty had preceded Orlando in the Amazon country and elsewhere in South America. Income from the Indian slave trade was once a major source of revenue, and between the years 1600 and 1650 no fewer than thirty expeditions to hunt Indians pushed deep into the heart of Brazil from the settlement now known as São Paulo.

In the following centuries, prospectors and others traveled again and again to the frontiers of the Chavantes, and the Indians vowed to defend themselves to the death against the newcomers. Up and down the land, Indians were carried off as captives—men, women, and children—and thousands of others died in epidemics of smallpox and other diseases brought by civilization. These epidemics have continued down to the present day and so have the wars with the Indians. The Indian population has been cut to one-sixth the size of four centuries ago.*

A friend of mine who recently retired from service in the United Nations gave a sample of the cruelty that has helped to form the South American Indians' feeling about white people. It happened in a disputed area in the borderland between Brazil and a neighboring country, to which he had been sent as an administrative officer for two years. When he reached his post, he asked the Indians how they felt about white people. "We cannot easily feel that you are our brothers," they told him. "We still remember when the rubber prospectors came. On Saturday nights, they would cover one of our men with kerosene and light it. As he ran through the dark to get to the river, they would try to shoot him."

* Much additional information on the racial history of Brazil, without which no student of South America could consider himself fully informed, can be found in the writings of Dr. Charles Wagley of Columbia University.

When Orlando planted himself in the center of the Xingu country, no other white man had ever settled there, for it was looked upon as one of the most dangerous parts of South America. Not long after he took up his life among the Indians, one tribe after another began to accept him as their friend and advisor.

He explained to me the two ways in which he made contact with hostile Indians. If he had won the friendship of an Indian who was in touch with a tribe, the Indian would help him to make the approach. But where warfare and distrust existed between the tribes, he would enter the territory of the hostile Indians and leave presents on the trail where they would find them. Steel knives and other tools were among the things most wanted by the jungle people, but he also left beads, fishhooks, mirrors, and other trinkets. Even chickens or other small animals have sometimes been used, for all people seem to be interested in pets. Later he would make his way again into the enemy country to see if the presents had been found. If they had been taken and nothing left in trade, he might leave more. But if this went on, it would be necessary to wait at the spot and try to draw the hostile group into peaceful relations. These Indians are generally quite ready to defend their territory, and there was always the danger of their attacking Orlando and driving him out. Even the small hunting parties of half a dozen or so Indians that one meets on the trail seem to have their leader, whose business it is to make decisions and command his fellows if there is a fight.

If the first meeting went well, Orlando would establish friendly trading. The dramatic moment always came when he undertook to enter the village of a new group. He was then quite at their mercy, being unarmed, greatly outnumbered, and sometimes even unsupported by his own Indians, whose presence might cause an outbreak between old enemies.

"Nothing really too bad," he said in his mild way. But most of us would describe it differently. It must sometimes have surprised those wild Indians, who thought only that their neighbors might rush in upon them, well armed and in great numbers, to see the lone figure of the little white man with the black beard standing at the edge of the clearing. In that moment a wave of the Chief's hand would tell the difference between a rain of arrows or a cautious approach to get a better look at the strange visitor. Orlando has had to flee for his life, but up to now the Indians have not brought him down or discouraged him from another try.

Orlando has gained a working knowledge of several Indian tongues, but there are many dialects in this part of South America, and he has often had to depend upon sign language. When he has established friendly relations with the chief of a tribe, there follows the task of making peace between warring groups. Here his powers of persuasion may meet their greatest test, because ancient quarrels are hard to stop. The only honorable thing for each of the feuding groups is to get "one up" on the other. And the Indians do not readily admit that their welfare depends upon burying the hatchet or that they can gain by trying peacefully to solve the common problems that face them all.

As news filtered back to Rio of this barefooted ambassador who passed unharmed through the jaws of danger, interest in him spread. The fact that his first thought seemed always to be for the Indians troubled those who felt that the interior could be developed better if the needs of the white man were considered first. Others saw in Orlando the key to a program with broader vision. And as his influence and his knowledge grew, the Indian Protective Service came to depend upon him more and more as its representative and to knit his work into its over-all program.

In our dugout were Orlando's younger brother, Cláudio, also a young captain in the Brazilian Air Force named Olavo Barreto Vianna whom I had met earlier in my travels, and two or three Indians. The river was broad, and the islands and bars of white sand had grown large with the advance of the dry season. On them eight-inch turtles were common, and there were many birds. At one bend in the river, at least sixty parrots flew up out of the trees at once. A good-sized alligator turned around on the sand and waddled into the river as we approached. Several times we saw giant river otters—they have been measured at over seven feet in length. More than once a canoe full of Indians passed us in the opposite direction 100 yards or more away.

Some three hours after leaving Jacaré, we turned into a river feeding the Kuluene from the wild country to the west. This was the Tuatuarí, on which a Camayurá village existed fairly near the mouth in 1948, though it is now apparently abandoned. It was a beautiful stream, clear as crystal, which twisted swift, smooth and deep among the palms. The water, despite its movement, was like glass. Near the bottom, which was for the most part clean sand, we could see fish swimming at a depth of eight or ten feet. But water plants were growing in places, which necessitated careful steering and rapid handling of the outboard to keep the propeller from getting fouled. In one of the beautiful pools we stopped and bathed. A finer swimming hole could not be found in any land.

It was about six in the evening when we beached the dugout and carried our baggage up the path to the village that is Orlando's headquarters.

Indians of four or five different tribes came out of their huts to meet us. The affection of the Indians for Orlando was a living proof that kindness can create harmony among the most opposite peoples and that a sympathetic heart does away with the need of bodyguards or treaties.

Several of the men in their twenties or thirties had no doubt been chosen by Orlando for the muscular strength they could give in building his headquarters. They were physically the most formidable Indians I had seen. Only about eight months had passed since this spot had been cleared for a village. The river was not visible from here, only the close circle of the forest.

We were arranging our baggage in Orlando's hut when a Hercules of an Indian appeared in the doorway—he was the champion intertribal wrestler—and told us we could eat. We went to a little thatched hut that served as kitchen and dining room. On a waist-high hearth of mud lay an armadillo, belly up, basking hideously on the embers. It was an easy animal to cook, because if left in its shell it didn't require any pan. We tore bits of the meat from the carcass, rolled them in pieces of manioc pancake the Indians had made, and ate them standing up. In a cauldron there were beans and rice in abundance. The coffee was excellent.

"Which were the most hostile Indians you ever met?" I asked Orlando.

"The Tumurí," he answered. "They live not far to the southwest of here, on the Rio Batoví, and are sometimes called the Xicão by the neighboring people. When we approached them, recently, they drove us back with a heavy attack of arrows. I have only this Tumurí war club and headdress, which we got from the village of a neighboring tribe whom they had attacked, killing many. We have not yet succeeded with the Tumurí, but we shall try again in a few months, leaving presents where they may find them to show that we wish them no harm."

"Were they worse than the Chavantes?" I asked.

"They came closer to killing us," said Orlando. "During the six months we spent crossing the Chavante country, the Indians only attacked or tried to attack twice, when we stopped to build an air strip. If we stopped for more than ten days, they apparently thought it strange, but there was no real danger. Then we had contact with the Juruna, but nothing serious happened there either, for we were prepared. They thought the meeting very strange, but they are Indians of good disposition. Later we came to the wild part of the Cajabí tribe, when we made the camp of the Rio Arinos. We were also successful there. North of here less than forty miles are the Suyá. They have not yet had any contact. We are now also trying to pacify the Tshukahamãe, a group farther down the Xingu. We have just come from this group. With them an additional problem exists, for they are in the habit of attacking the rubber gatherers farther down the Xingu. We actually convinced the tribe that it would be to their advantage to have an airstrip in their territory, which would put them in touch with the metal tools and medical help they need."

[On a later visit to this tribe, Cláudio found part of them still willing to have the airstrip but the rest eager to kill him. Even so, he was able to clear the strip. Ground gained and partly lost again; that is the story of progress in the wilderness of the Xingu.]

"Do you think the hostility of the Indians against civilized people is the result of old grievances," I asked, "or are some of the Indians simply more warlike by nature?"

"Mostly because of grievances. Here on the upper Xingu, where the Indians have had little contact with white people, they have warred with each other but not against us."

The Xingu Indians had killed quite a few white people, and I mentioned this.

"But these killings had special causes, understandable to anyone knowing the customs of the people and their desire to protect their own territory. These killings happened before the Indian Protective Service brought the policies of General Rondon to the area."

Recalling how Genésio Pimentel Barbosa and his five men had not even reached for their guns when the Chavantes slaughtered them, I ventured to say that the cost had been heavy.

"Undeniably, many have lost their lives, but no other way has been possible, and today we follow exactly the humanitarian ethics of General Rondon—respect for the culture of the Indians, their social organization, their customs, their family life, and their religion."

We finished the meal in almost total darkness, and Orlando returned to his hut to write up some of the notes of his trip. He seated himself on a rough stool he had made, which was covered with the spotted skin of a jaguar, and wrote in a notebook on his knee with a finely sharpened lead pencil. His page was lighted by a kerosene lantern hanging from the thatched roof. Near him was a packing box he had made into a bookcase. From time to time he would remove a paper-bound volume from it, consult it, and put it back in its place. I suppose the three shelves would have totaled eight or ten feet of books, almost entirely technical. In the center of the bookcase was a worn copy of the Bible.

Presently a little Indian boy came in and sat on Orlando's free knee. Then I saw the arm of another Indian boy go around his neck, and there was hardly room on his shoulder for a parrot that flew down and perched there. Under his legs, a bird almost as large as a turkey kept bothering him for attention, which it received every few minutes. A long low dog something like a dachshund lay with its chin on one of his bare feet. An Indian woman came to be treated for a small injury, and Orlando bandaged it.

I had lain down while Orlando was treating her, and I must have closed my eyes, for when I looked up he was gone. I couldn't believe he had slipped out past me, and I peered into all the shadows in the hut trying to find him—in the corner where the broken guitar stood, around the walls where the Indian masks, war clubs, and bows and arrows hung. He wasn't sitting on the expedition chest under the lifebelts he used when descending rapids, or over by the medicine cabinets. Then I heard a sound from high on one wall, right under the thatching of the roof. There was a little hammock about the size of the one provided for clothing in a Pullman berth; Orlando had climbed into it and was reading an adventure story in a two-year-old magazine.

Orlando kept his detailed diary of his travels partly as the duty of a man in virgin territory learning things that could never be gotten again with the same freshness, and partly through his personal interest in the ways of the strange people of the jungle. He also needed to record times and distances so as to plot his way on a later journey. But when I asked him whether he thought of writing a book of his adventures, he said no, that he was only interested in putting the scientific facts on record.

The Villas Boas brothers, in all their years in the jungle, had not taken on the toughness that some men like to show as proof that the wilderness is theirs. They had perfect manners. Neither of them had ever married, though the Indian Service, for which they now worked, would not have discouraged them from having wives. However, the girl who would enjoy the sort of life that Orlando had cut out for himself would be a rare one, and he hardly ran much chance of finding her where he was. The Indian Service would not have approved his marrying an Indian, which is an interesting attitude in a country that has always been noted for its open-mindedness about mixed marriages.

No country in the world has taken intermixture more in its stride than Brazil. There is exceptional freedom from racial prejudice. The early colonists from Portugal were mostly men, and the Portuguese crown encouraged marriages with the Indians. By the end of the eighteenth century, people of mixed European and Indian ancestry formed a sizable part of the population. Great numbers of Negro slaves were imported, and intermarriage continued, with abundant additions from various European and Asiatic countries. The Brazilians are not unaware of racial differences, but there is greater freedom to discuss them than with us. Far from opposing interracial marriage, the Brazilians become concerned when one group keeps to itself. But in the case of these "unspoiled" Indians, the Indian Protective Service and other interested groups have made an about-face. There had been quite a stir when one employee of the Indian Service and another in the Central Brazilian Foundation married Indian girls from this region. In one instance, the marriage was dissolved; in the other, the argument came to a sad end when the bride died in childbirth.

Cláudio, the youngest brother, had been described to me as a "priest" who had never taken the cloth and as an extremely self-contained man. But I saw neither of these aspects of his personality, though he was quieter and more studious than Orlando. He had read much of the scientific literature of the Amazon and its people. Although he often let his brother answer first, he generally talked freely on any subject I brought up. Neither of them had lost an interest in the affairs of the world. But the easiest question I asked them during my stay was whether they thought of going back to civilization. They both laughed at once and said no. Leonardo, the third brother, was stationed far to the northeast on the big island in the Araguaia River, Ilha do Bananal.

That night we strung our hammocks outside at the edge of the forest. They told me they had seen a jaguar not ten yards from where they had slept a few nights before. I could not share their apparent unconcern over this fact, but the night passed peacefully.

CHAPTER XXIII

WHICH WAY THE TRAIL?

It was in this village, around the campfire at night, that I was able to get additional recordings of native music. Its exotic quality has moved audiences wherever I have played it, and its importance in the long story of mankind is the greater because so few places are left on earth where art forms that are truly primitive can still be captured.

Diseases brought in by civilized people have dealt staggering blows to primitive people. The first known epidemic of measles in Alaska, which struck early in this century, killed as many as 75 per cent of the Eskimos in some villages. At least 25 per cent died wherever it struck, and in one village on the Kuskokwim River only one person survived out of 99. Smallpox, tuberculosis, and venereal disease have also brought disaster. I asked Orlando whether there was any way to protect the Xingu Indians against these losses.

"On first contact," he said, "the effect is disastrous. An epidemic of measles would be a calamity here. But the Indian Protective Service creates an iron belt around the region, so that the civilized person who enters is carefully screened. The Indians of this region do not have one case of tuberculosis. Measles, chickenpox, smallpox, and mumps are unknown. They suffer only from malaria and epidemics of grippe. Against these, our drugs work wonders."*

* As this goes to press, word comes that a measles epidemic is sweeping the tribes of the upper Xingu. About one-third of the Camayurá tribe have died. The relief efforts of the Indian Protective Service were handicapped when one of their planes was wrecked on an airstrip. It is estimated that half of the Camayurás will succumb before the disease can be halted.

“[illegible]hat science can safeguard these people agai[illegible]s?”

“A[illegible]ord shows that it is worth trying. Take the B[illegible]le, to the southwest of here. Originally there [illegible]m. Today there are 150. In only fifty years, 4,850 died. For the pleasure of being converted to our ways and beliefs, they paid a heavy price. If you go among the Bororos today, you will hear them playing our religious music beautifully on trumpets and clarinets. You will not see them dance their traditional dances, nor do they fish or hunt or farm. They keep on dying easily and being buried to the music of the clarinet.”

Clearly Orlando, in his work with the Indians, was leaving their religious philosophy alone. I mentioned that in my travels as an anthropologist I had seen mission schools, colleges, and hospitals that I thought were of great help to backward people. I also said that I had seen missionaries blamed for harm that had been caused by traders, trappers, prospectors, and others.

Orlando thought a moment. Then he said, “The question of the missionary is difficult. One could not deny, for example, that a missionary of good will with medical help can aid the Indian. In comparison with the riffraff of the frontier—certain diamond prospectors, rubber men, and the like—the missionary is far superior. But when the missionary indoctrinates the Indians in regard to their spiritual and religious life, all parts of their culture are altered and a process of decay sets in. One thing affects all the others. We have the example of the contact of the missionaries with the Meináco [a tribe to the south]. That was a great stupidity and a bad lesson. The Meináco Indians, under the influence of the missionaries, gave up a great part of their ceremonial life, and their culture was disturbed in such a way that a breakdown began. Finally, without anyone influencing them, they reacted against the missionaries and stopped accepting their teach[illegible]ly after they had suffered the damage. Here t[illegible]not been harmed in this way. If missionaries [illegible]om that moment the Indians will suffer har[illegible]mis-sionaries upset their social organization. [illegible] the missionary is better than the riffraff."

I wondered whether Orlando migh[illegible] the Indians only to have them worse exploit[illegible] the end. Contact with the outside world seemed u[illegible]voidable. No one could foretell when mineral treasures might be found here, and then the stampede would be on. It is interesting to compare this situation with our own in the United States. Our reservations were set up after most of the Indians had been crowded back into smaller space than they had been used to. They were then persuaded to settle for less territory in return for special privileges, including tax exemption on their land holdings. Orlando wanted to reserve this land solely for the Indians who had lived naturally on it since before the coming of white people. That gave him a better chance of securing the Indians' good will and of working out a program of transition. Today in the United States, almost 170 years after the reservation policy was set up, there is still trouble when the Indian wants to leave his tribal land and enter the life of the nation with the rest of us. Reservation life has not yet made our Indians ready for the change. When 1,575 members of the Flathead tribe in Montana were given the right to dispose of their land, it wasn't long before less than one out of a hundred still had any. Even where it is only a question of leasing the water rights or mineral rights, our Indians have fallen into the hands of ruthless lawyers, politicians, and promoters. The weak point in all trusteeships over native peoples (and this is a problem that affects our reputation in all parts of the world) is the difficulty of carrying through a plan of development that will enable the natives, within a reasonable period of time, to manage their own affairs and yet fit into the economic and political life around them.

In our own country at this time, some of the most revolutionary laws ever suggested were being presented in Congress. Ten bills in the making would end federal responsibility for more than 66,000 Indians in ten states. These laws would free the government from its existing duties regarding the health and education of the Indians and deprive them of the tax exemption on their property. Other tribes were fearing that the laws would be the opening wedge for similar treatment of them.

As Orlando talked, I thought how simple it would be for unscrupulous people to get the better of the Xingu Indians. (Within three months from that day, "land grabbers" dared to massacre 22 Chavantes in order to steal from them.)

"The wave of civilization will come, you know," I said. "Do you really believe that these people can rise with it instead of being drowned by it?"

For the first time, something almost fierce came into him. "It is our whole aim to save them," he said. "Naturally, they will not always have it like this. But they must not jump from their culture into ours, unless we want to see them become like the poorest laborer, afflicted with tuberculosis and intestinal parasites, miserable in spirit and hopeless in outlook. The change must be gradual, and they must have perfect help all along."

I knew how costly the kind of help he meant would be. There was a sympathy for the Indian in Brazil not generally present in most countries. But it would be a heavy drain on the public treasury to put into action the program of protection and education this would involve. "I'd feel better," I said, "if the Indians were producing something for civilized economy, so that they could help pay the bill."

"Ah, great progress is being made by the Indian Protective Service," said Orlando, and he went on to give the figures.

The Indians of South Brazil in 1952 had produced $80,000 worth of wheat and $67,500 worth of wood. The Mundurucú Indians of the state of Pará produced $16,500 worth of rubber, and so on. In 1950, the total value of Indian production was only $34,705. The next year, when Dr. José M. de Gama Malcher became director of the Indian Protective Service, it rose to $139,800, and in 1952 it reached $198,700. Some Indians who were quite wild only two years ago and were killing rubber collectors were now producing.

"How about these Xingu tribes?" I asked.

"Alas, we have no natural products here to extract—no diamonds, no rubber, no Brazil nuts."

"The hammocks these Indians make are beautiful and useful," I suggested. "They could be sold in Rio and even in the United States."

"A good idea," Orlando nodded. "And they are light enough to be shipped out by airplane. There are also fur-bearing animals—the *onça* [jaguar] and giant otter—but to take them would be contrary to the creation of a national preserve to protect the Indians and their world."

I asked more about this national preserve, and Orlando's eyes lighted. "It is the only hope for these people," he said. "All over the world there are preserves to protect the animals but none to protect the Indians and their culture. This will be the center."

Glancing around the clearing, it was hard to imagine how this spot on the edge of nowhere could become the center of anything.

"Come with me," he said, and he led me along a path through the jungle.

As we walked, I learned more of his hope to establish an administrative and scientific headquarters for all the tribes of the Xingu, under the Indian Service.

Ninety-seven posts of the Indian Service already exist throughout Brazil. Some of them can only be reached by plane. Some of the others that are serviced by river boats are cut off for nine months of the year by low water. The men in these outposts are exposed to many dangers. Shortly before I left Rio, the men at the Trucará post, less than 200 miles from Belém, had been attacked repeatedly by the Paracanã Indians. The white men had settled first in a roofless enclosure in the forest, where they had little protection from arrows. Then they found themselves cut off without food or trade goods. Some supplies were got to them, and they built a cabin. Then they tried to open relations through interpreters, but the Indians only shot arrows at them. One day when the men were attacked while eating lunch, they gathered the arrows, tied them in a bundle, and left them with presents where the Indians would find them. The Paracanãs attacked again, using even larger arrows. While the men were pulling them out of the wall, they kept calling out, hoping to get a friendly answer from the Indians. Forty-five arrows were gathered and placed like the others on the trail, with manioc flour and knives.

Finally the Indians approached and said they could not understand clearly. The white men might well have made this complaint, because the Paracanãs pierce the lower lip and wear a piece of wood in it, which hampers their speech. They were described as medium-sized Indians with a tan complexion and, strangely, a very ample beard and mustache. The men kept saying, "*Caraiba catù* (white man good)," and gradually the Indians grew more trustful. On May 9, six of them came to the post; on the 14th, eight; and on the 18th, eleven.*

Three times as many posts are needed, yet the Indian Protective Service is limited to the budget laid down in 1940, when the Brazilian currency would buy more than it does now. It is unfortunate that the men of the Brazilian Indian Service, who win admiration throughout the world for their courage, resourcefulness, and good will, have to work for so little. Some of the employees receive only $400 a year, which is scarcely half the minimum wage required by law. The man in charge of a center in a state, with fifteen years of experience, receives only $1,720.

The Indian Service does wonders with only two medical doctors, who range over a territory as large as the United States. Of course they can't visit all of the 1,000 or more native villages. Estimates of the Indian population of Brazil vary from 200,000 to 1,000,000 (Dr. Malcher thinks there are about 400,000), and some seventy different dialects are spoken. The more important posts have dispensaries and nurses, and a radio network keeps the Rio office informed of emergencies and epidemics. The Service operates sixty schools. The Brazilians look upon their Indian Protective Service as the first institution in America to aid the Indians with the idea of protection rather than religious conversion. Its avowed policy is the positivism of General Rondon, who at 87 still presides over the National Council that guides its programs.

Along the coast, most of the Indians have been eliminated in the advance of civilization. In the northeast, hardly 6,000 remain. The great majority are in the Amazon Basin, and the wildest, least-known part is northern Mato Grosso—Orlando's

* From accounts published in *Correio da Manha* (March 27, 1953) and *O Globo* (May 24, 1953).

beat. The post that he was setting up here in the Xingu was to be called the Capitão Vasconcelos Post in honor of the man who headed the Rondon Commission into the region in 1922 and stimulated scientific and humanitarian interest in it.

After a short walk through the forest, we came out into full sunlight and were looking at a perfectly level airfield two-thirds of a mile long.

"How did you ever do it?" I asked.

"Not hard if the Indians are with you," he said. "At times as many as 1,000, belonging to various tribes and speaking different languages, have gathered to help us. The problem of feeding them all is difficult. Local Indians must be persuaded to feed the visitors. Tribes unknown to each other trade, all for the mutual advantage."

There are times when Orlando has had more time than facilities or materials with which to advance his program. But he invariably rises before sun-up, and when the medicines run short he has to try to tell the real invalids from the imaginary ones. Meanwhile, he has nursed himself through repeated attacks of malaria. His skin is peppered with thousands of little black pinpoints from the stings of mosquitoes.

"This will be the hub of the wheel," he said. "Seven other airfields in different directions will enable us to circulate supplies, medical services, mail, and the like. Several of them are already in good shape, all the way from Rio Verde in the west to the Rio das Mortes in the east and north to the border of Pará." On a map he outlined the territory that would lie within the Preserve of the Xingu, an area of about 99,000 square miles. Roughly the southeastern third of it would be only provisional, but portions of it would be incorporated into the Preserve when the occupying tribes were pacified.

"The law, if passed, will protect the land and all its resources for the Indian tribes. The Preserve will remain their inalienable homeland, not to be divided or parceled out to others. There will be no trespassing in their territory without permission from a special council made up of the highest federal scientific institutions and of the Historical and Geographical Institute of Mato Grosso. The plant and animal life of the region will be protected and studied scientifically. The bill provides for five million cruzeiros [about $125,000] for a period of five years, to cover setting up our headquarters and outlying survey stations, complete with airports, radio stations, observation posts, and lodging for scientists. Over here will be the medical hut; there, the supply hut; and beyond, the radio station. All around, there will be huts for visiting tribes, where they can stay while sharing their dances and other ceremonies. And while we are looking after their needs, scientists can study the culture of the various tribes of the region, so that we can find out about the origin of these people while their life is yet unchanged."

The little man with the bare feet and the eyes of a prophet had a big idea, yet I wondered whether he was not already thinking of deeper wildernesses to conquer. He is almost the opposite of our North American go-getter, who is always eager to implement the total potential and maximize the impact. He has become part of the jungle. He can roll with its punches. Yet when a swift stab is called for, as when a luxury airliner crashed in the jungle some hundreds of miles away, he can move with the speed, skill, and stamina of a jungle-born Indian.

Watching him with the Indians, I doubted that he knew why they liked him. His approach was unstudied, and I couldn't tell whether there had ever been a time when he had needed to adopt any rules of behavior. Somehow he had become interested in these folk of the forest and had taken up living among them because he liked them, not because he wanted to make them like himself. He would have been the despair of a do-gooder. Yet even an evangelist might pause to wonder about the dreams of a man who had so little to sell.

Orlando's methods are unlike those of our big corporations which, admitting an enlightened self-interest, set up an island of hospitals, swimming pools, and recreation houses in the wilderness before talking wages and hours with the local labor force. When they have dented the frontier, Orlando will already be far beyond it—one man in nature's broadest domain.

I wondered whether he would have patience enough to wait for the help he needed—and whether his luck would hold. Would the arrow find its mark the next time he tried to meet the Tumurí, or those nameless people beyond? His own friendly Indians right here in the Kuluene would almost certainly in some measure turn against him when the pleasures and opportunities of civilization began to tempt them. How could one man keep them from crossing so many miles of unguarded boundary? Orlando had absolute power to forbid them to go. No plane could take an Indian on board without his approval. But the ways of escape would grow more numerous.

We strolled back to his encampment. Orlando swept his hand around and said, "When we finish the other buildings in a few months, all this will be burned to the ground."

"But will the bill really be passed; will the Preserve be established?" I asked.

"It must be," he said. "The President is in favor of it, and so are other influential people in the government. It can't fail. It mustn't."

It was the last night in Orlando's hut. We were stringing our hammocks, and it was a bit crowded.

"Ah, well," he said, "next year our new main hut will be finished, and there will be plenty of room."

"Running water in every room?" I asked.

"Naturally," said Orlando with a laugh, "and coffee served in the hammock every morning."

CHAPTER XXIV

THE MEEK AND THE MIGHTY

Not many hours later, I had traveled back down the Kuluene and was on the long flight home—thirty hours flying time from stone-age jungle to twentieth-century New York City.

Our Pan American air ship was somewhere over the endless tangled wilderness of the Amazon north of Rio de Janeiro when the stewardess handed me a chicken dinner, with champagne. The American businessmen near me were talking about the price of cotton in Uruguay.

The sun was setting outside my porthole. There was a thread of smoke directly beneath us, rising straight toward heaven for half a mile in the evening air. Far over toward the horizon was another thin column of smoke, probably a week away by jungle trail.

The evening fires had been lighted down there in that ancient other world beneath the matted forest, and I could picture it all. I could hear the flutes, smell the *urucú* paint, and feel the ground shake to the thumping sticks. Pat-pat, smile, pat-pat. The fires were crackling in the huts; the mothers were blowing warm air on their babies in the hammocks. The macaws were settling themselves for the night.

Back over our rudder, 500 miles away and seemingly 10,000 years ago, was that strong little man who had found the Land of Long Ago and had but one thought—to stay there until he made the world a better place for the jungle Indians. A big order.

Too old-fashioned to suit the city fathers, too new for the planners? A prophet ahead of his time, an enigma, a white god, a phantom. Be this as it may, we can be sure that far and wide through the thick forest—beyond the difficult crossing, above the rapids, over the divide—men of the jungle speaking many tongues will say, "He passed this way and was known to be kind."

Charles Darwin, though we think of him in connection with the doctrine of the survival of the fittest, was by all accounts a gentle and kindly soul. Even when describing the struggle for existence in the animal world, he pointed out that progress often depended upon mutual assistance. But the world in his day was moving toward two world wars, and the minds of men were ruled by the need to win a physical struggle against an enemy. People borrowed part of Darwin's doctrine, at least unconsciously, to bolster the philosophy that might makes right. And when in 1902 a geographer named Prince Kropotkin wrote a book called *Mutual Aid*, which showed that many creatures survive and prosper through co-operation, it scarcely made a ripple on the surface. For as man gained sudden mastery over the materials and energies of the natural world, he found it ever easier to believe that peace could be gained only through greater wars.

Yet some in every age have said that neither body nor brain can carry us upward. It will be a mysterious force, they say—not the strength that won supremacy for the dinosaurs in their time nor the wizardry of machines through which we of today seek to make ourselves secure, but a quite different force, a growth of the spirit. The opposite of the belief that might makes right would be that the strong shall help the weak; indeed that the meek shall prevail over the mighty. I like the French phrasing better: "Blessed are the debonair." For today the word "meek" sounds long-suffering and spiritless, whereas the debonair, aside from being gentle in disposition, are affable and courteous, graceful and gay. The word fits in some measure my jungle brothers, the Camayurás. They have inherited a beautiful part of the world. They could go on living there for thousands of years, just as they have in the past, if they had no contact with us. But as soon as they meet us, it will take something that we do not possess to save them. Perhaps it is because we are not always gentle and good, affable and courteous, not to mention graceful and gay.

I am describing a trail that is ever so much more difficult than getting to the center of South America and back. It is harder to tell where you are on this trail. The people who inherit the earth won't even know they have it. There was that little man in his bare feet and ragged trousers whose word was law throughout a country as big as our six northeastern states, yet he didn't really know what he had, except a piece of work that he liked very much.

We were only an hour from Idlewild Airport when I had an attack of superstition. I think it was a reaction to having had so much good luck. It was as though I had already had several lives and was living on borrowed time. I felt that the law of averages was against me, and I grew anxious about the landing.

Then I reflected that if you have something and are afraid of losing it, you haven't got it. And I stopped worrying.

Presently we were coming in to the runway, and next I was walking toward my own people. There was Fenley Hunter, who found that 23,800-year-old stone point in Nevada, and his wife Hazel (who found a tooth the size of a pinhead that belonged to a 22-million-year-old field mouse). There was my brother who would live in Athens in the age of Pericles, and his wife Mina who would add to the gaiety of nations in any age. There was Blackie, who, like all dogs since the first one who came in out of the forest to help civilize man, asked no questions about absence but only rejoiced in reunion. There was Susie, who, quietly worrying all those weeks, might be said to have learned more about what the Chavantes can do to you than any of us. And there was Rodi, who had been nine when I left but was now ten.

"Tell us what it was like, Daddy?" Rodi said.

This book is my effort to answer that question. I have tried to give you as faithful a narrative as I could. But there are still many mysteries to be solved.